Stoicism

Understanding and Practicing the Philosophy of the Stoics

Stoicism

Understanding and Practicing the Philosophy of the Stoics

Your Guide to Wisdom, Freedom, Happiness, and Living the Good Life

Kyle Faber

Stoicism – Understanding and Practicing the Philosophy of the Stoics

Published by CAC Publishing LLC
ISBN: 978-1-950010-25-7 paperback
ISBN: 978-1-950010-24-0 eBook

This book is dedicated to those that truly wish to live the good life. Stoicism is not about money or fancy things, it's about living your best life regardless of what's around you. To escape the daily pressures and bland existence we trap ourselves in.

Table of Contents

Conclusion 210

Introduction

"Only the educated are free."

— Epictetus

Stoicism is a deep and penetrating topic that does not lend itself to rapid instruction and shallow practice. Its nuances and complexities are best absorbed gradually and with deliberate attention paid to the details. Understanding Stoicism can't be done at arm's length by instruction alone. It requires a two-way connection between the teacher and the student. The teacher lays out the philosophy in gradual steps, and the student absorbs it, reflects on it, practices it, and then builds on it before putting it all together in his or her own mind.

It is nothing like a recipe where one starts with the ingredients, follows the steps, and places it in the oven and voilà a cake appears. Stoicism is not dessert. It is a philosophy, and it is also a way of life that comes from an internal fountain and is in harmony with external forces. For something to be a way of life, you have to live it, and you have to experiment with it and adapt it to your personal situation.

If you are expecting a book that is going to be a step-by-step how-to book that will somehow miraculously transform your state of mind to a Stoic's state of existence, then you will face disappointment early. You should, instead, be prepared to go much deeper, treading slowly, pausing at each incremental stage to acclimate yourself.

The goal of this book is to reveal the soul of the Stoic and methods by which that soul forms so that one may chart a path toward that outcome. The book does not presume any prior knowledge of Stoicism. Come as you are. It is what it is, and so whether you are a student of Greek philosophy or a total novice interested in bringing peace into your life, this book places you on the path you need to make it so.

The two intellectual giants of Western civilization—the Greeks and the Romans—provided the reservoir of observations, advice, and understanding of the human soul, the nature of the universe, and how the two collide. It is embodied in the sea of work that resulted in such philosophies as Stoicism. The pursuit of Stoic philosophy today is just as relevant as it was back then simply because we are all searching for the truth, and the best way to ascertain that truth is to be able to develop a framework in which to observe it, practice it, and internalize it.

Chapter 1 - Framework of Stoic Philosophy

"Everything we hear is an opinion, not a fact. Everything we see is a perspective, not the truth."

— Emperor Marcus Aurelius Antoninus Augustus, 180 AD

Around 300 BC, just after the death of Alexander the Great, the intellectual influence that straddled the region stretching from the Mediterranean to the foot of the Himalayan range was propelled by the momentum that came with the Hellenistic conquest of the region.

From the farthest extent of Aryan lands in northern India to the architectural wonders of Babylon in West Asia, Alexander had spread an intellectual curiosity that gave rise to the amalgamation and acceptance of Western philosophies that eventually resulted in the amalgamation and proliferation of Western civilization.

As the Hellenistic age prepared to advance and breathe life into the Roman Republic and then into Imperial Rome, a new breed of thinkers emerged and brought with them the foundations of an old philosophy to take on new roots. They started to identify and answer questions surrounding life living, and through dialectic processes formulated a series of philosophical guardrails, grammatical rules, and ideological tenets that formed the framework of a key school of thought that would go on to become the basis of the grammar we use in communication today, the process of inquiry that is the basis to develop science and technologies, and also as the basis of major religions.

To be clear, this was not just the work of one man but rather a collaborative effort that started at the steps of the Agora in post-Socratic times (some will argue, earlier) and developed all the way to Emperor Marcus Aurelius' palace in Rome. Much of the philosophy that resulted was rooted in the arguments and ideas that transpired among men of crystal-clear thought and rock-solid virtue. They attempted to distill from collaborative life lessons a body of knowledge that would clearly and succinctly become the keys to inner peace and wisdom and the means by which they could conquer it.

What resulted from this intellectual cauldron was a set of virtues unheard of until that time and which came to be known as Stoicism. Those who practiced it came to famously be known as Stoics.

In ancient Greece, the word "Stoic" didn't exist as any verb or noun. The leading philosophies and schools of thought of the day were named according to the place in which the teachers of that philosophy gathered to exchange ideas and information. So, if today, you got together at your local library's porch to discuss your particular philosophy, it would come to be known as the "Porch Philosophy." In the same way, the thinkers of the intellectual philosophy used to congregate at the portico at the Agora in Athens, and so it came to be known as the philosophy of the painted portico. In Greek, that is called *"Stoa Poikile."* You can see how that gradually morphed into Stoic and on to Stoicism.

Stoic represents the person, while Stoa or Stoicism represents the philosophy.

The intellectual giants of the period, including Socrates; his students Plato, Euclid, and Xenophon; and their students, such as Aristotle, discussed various ideas over the course of a century, from the time of Socrates, circa 400 BC, to the time of Zeno's founding of Stoicism in 301 BC, a century of debate and reflection by men of towering intellect distilling what we now regard as this philosophy of the Stoics.

If nothing else, it should tell you that the philosophy we are looking at is something that has been synthesized and distilled by some of the most intellectual minds of the classical era over a significant period of time. It is a decidedly cerebral and sober observation of the nature of all things and the harmonious course of action, which is easily adaptable to today's world.

As Greek dominance gave way to Roman hegemony and Roman influence spread to the provinces, the philosophical center of gravity shifted to the amphitheaters in Rome. Here, the likes of Seneca the Younger and the sixteenth emperor of the Roman Empire, Marcus Aurelius, adopted the philosophy and propelled it forward, allowing it to gain traction and mainstream attention.

If you were thinking that Stoicism began in Rome, just know that that is a common fallacy. It actually started in Greece and moved to Rome over time to become the mores of the educated, not the religion of the masses.

Early Religions

While Stoicism is not a religion, comparing it to religions prevalent in those times has its advantages and its limits. Philosophers taught students how to think, not what to think. In essence, philosophy paved the way for the student to discover the truth. Religion does the same thing but goes one step further. It allows the human mind to project outward to a higher being, and that being becomes the personification of all things that the human mind cannot comprehend or undertake. It served a powerful purpose. It became the catchall of all unknowns.

For instance, in the days of early marine endeavors, as the Greeks boarded their triremes for war on distant shores, they had no concept of weather, climate, tide, and wind. They could not predict what the elements would do once the fleet set sail. They didn't know about weather fronts moving over the area or about pressure systems causing heavy rain or strong winds. They didn't understand the basic mechanics of wind and tide above what they could easily observe. They left what they didn't know to the whims of the gods. In other words, what the human mind could not comprehend but still observe, it ascribed to one almighty hidden force. To conform to the human mind, they personified that force and called it God.

From there, the God of Sea, the God of War, the God of the Sun, and others were brought forth. Those deities formed the early multigod universe, which then evolved into a unitary and almighty god universe that was adopted by the new religion of Christianity that took hold during the time of Emperor Constantine.

Many wars also resulted from religious roots, which can be taken as further proof that religion serves as the wild card—whenever we don't understand something, including our emotional hostility, political hostility, and seeming differences—we assign and ascribe it to religion, just as the Greek sailors ascribed climatology to invisible gods.

Religions back then were divided across two camps: ones that symbolized and were personified by deities—the manifestation of the mind's observation and the desire to worship what humans thought were the powers that ruled over them. Worship was both an attempt to pay adulation to the gods to curry favor and also to ask for things they wanted that seemed beyond their own grasp.

The second kind of religion involved nature. Naturalists and pagan worshipers reflected the thought of the power of nature over humans. As the church took hold in later centuries, it became outlawed and looked down upon. Many of these practitioners of nature worship were labeled as heretics and witches and eventually killed at the stake.

By the time the Greeks had brought religion into the mainstream, they were also pursuing intellectual paths that were the product of rational thought. It seemed then and still does now that religion and rational thought occupied opposite ends of nature's spectrum.

To get a wide-ranging picture, it is also wise to touch briefly on the issue of spirituality, which is not the same as theology, and those who are agnostic or atheists by choice would typically tend to gravitate toward spirituality at some point and find that it has more to offer than the theology of organized religions.

That is to be expected, and you can visualize this with something more common. Think about food. Think about how food is prepared when it is done by a chef for just a small family. Consider the amount of time and care that goes into the preparation and the level of individualization that it can afford. On the other hand, if you were buying preprepared, mass-produced food, what you would get is something highly mechanized, highly processed, and significantly less nutritious. Philosophies are the same way. When you take time and focus on something in philosophy and religion and do it over a long period of time, you find that it takes on an organic flavor. However, when you mass-produce a religion, it has a more processed flavor and ends up leaving a bad taste in your mouth.

One way to approach this tapestry is to see that spirituality is not as heavy on dogma as religion is; religion is not as heavy on logic and reasoning as philosophy is, and philosophy is not as ethereal as spirituality. When you see it this way, what you will also see if you pull your focus back is that they are all part of a seamless tapestry that exists in three dimensions.

This book is concerned only with the philosophical aspect of this tapestry, and more specifically it is only focusing on the philosophy of the Stoics. Numerous other philosophies exist, and all of them have something to offer their students. As you will see in the chapter on historical roots, many of these philosophies find their genesis in the logic and thinking of Socrates a hundred years before. You will also see that we all exist on a spectrum. Nothing is distinctly different from something else, for example, Stoics have similarities to Cynics, who have similarities to Epicureans, who have similarities to academicians.

The religion, culture, and thinking of Greece evolved and was transplanted during the inception of Rome by Romulus and Remus. In its early days, Greece was a loose construct of city-states stretching from the Aegean Sea to the eastern shores of the Mediterranean. One of the largest of these cities was Troy. Upon the siege of Troy and its eventual sacking and razing, the inhabitants who survived, however few, left the burning city and made their way on foot to Italy. One of these people was a man by the name of Aeneas. Under his leadership, the former citizens of Troy set up a new village. In short order, the descendants of this village were transplanted to another city that was created on the slopes of Mount Alba, which they named

Alba Longa. This city is where Romulus and Remus, founders of Rome, were born.

The teachings, philosophy, religions, culture, and technology made a clear and direct path from the fragmented city-states of Greece into the fabric of Rome from the very first moment of its birth.

The religion and academics of Greece were part of the soul of Rome. While the teachings in Rome evolved as the city was gradually being built and maturing, parallels in their thinking evolved as well. The elites in Rome not only learned to read and speak Latin but were also inclined to study Greek so that they could tap into the intellectual veins of resources rooted in Athens in particular and Greece as a whole in general.

Men like Julius Caesar and some of the emperors after him were schooled in Greek literature and philosophy, and that formed the intellectual basis of the Roman mind-set. At the same time, the Roman age and the expansion of the empire allowed the proliferation of ideas and ideals across the provinces.

As religions took hold, it was a form of hope that spread across the masses like wildfire. It was a psychological panacea to almost any difficulty that was prevalent, and it allowed the citizens of Greece and Rome to postpone today's pain in hopes of tomorrow's potential. That was the key to every religion. Whether it was the desire for revenge or good fortune or even the need for a larger-than-life protector for whatever seemed like a larger-than-life threat, religion gave the ancient masses access to an all-powerful being that could make it happen.

From the perspective of theological history, religions served a particular purpose to alleviate pain and give hope. This theology was hijacked and weaponized by politics and politicians. When Rome was on the cusp of imperialism and Caesar had just been murdered by those close to him, it happened to be a time when Hailey's Comet was coming into view. It proved to be the perfect time for Caesar's nephew and adopted heir, Octavius, to point to the sky and tell the world that what they saw in the sky was his uncle rising to heaven to take his seat as a god.

The trickery worked. The public believed it, and they started to see Julius as a deity and Octavian, who later renamed himself Augustus, as the son of a god. It was a brilliant political ploy that worked. The people of Rome then went on to beg and force Augustus to become emperor. He actually never asked for the job, and, in fact, he shunned it at first, which made them want him to be emperor even more. Augustus gave the masses hope as the son of god and became the earthly nexus to heavenly power. Not too far from where that was happening a young boy was born, who grew up to become a carpenter, and was claiming the same thing.

We see across civilizations and time that the need for a superhuman being manifests in many ways, and some grow popular enough to become a religion. There is definitely a place for religious dogma and teachings in the tapestry of the human condition. It is a small part of understanding a complex and multidimensional universe, but it isn't the be all and end all that it is sometimes considered to be. As mentioned earlier in the book, there is a three-dimensional tapestry of truth that is stretched across religion, philosophy, and spirituality. Without truly understanding religion, however foreign it may be to our own mind-set, we are robbed of the diversity of thought that eventually assists in the understanding of truth.

Understanding it is as important to the future development of the mind as the development of internal peace that one feels when knowing that they have something greater than themselves to handle difficulties that can seem greater than their individual might.

Stoicism addresses this tapestry perfectly because it has hidden religious and spiritual aspects that make it one of the most comprehensive philosophies that give you a better picture of the truth. It also ends up giving you a better framework to develop the ability to experience the truth within yourself. In other words, Stoicism straddles the center of balance in the philosophical, religious, and spiritual tapestry.

Religious Nature of Stoicism

Not all Stoicism is about religion or spirituality, but it has features of Christianity, Deism, Buddhism, and other major religions. It may be hard for those of you who are agnostic or atheistic to even consider the notion that such similarities exist with organized religion and the philosophy of Stoicism. Stoic philosophy does not discount the existence of an all-powerful force of creation. In essence, this force is monolithic and unitary in the same way that Christianity is monotheistic and suggests an omnipotent and omnipresent god.

Stoicism is constantly asking a larger question, which is more than just about being stoic or pensive in nature. The larger question that Stoics and Christians ask is related to the purpose of one's life.

Stoics are constantly attempting to delve deeper into the root of existence and the need to make that existence worthwhile. It turns out that just as Socrates and Heraclitus had suspected and observed a life that is spent in pursuit of a greater purpose is one that works out better. In Christianity, the purpose of life has been to serve God, and a life that is devoted to that purpose is one that was considered blessed.

Like similarities between Stoicism and Christianity, there are also similarities between Stoic observations and Buddhist teachings. Although they both evolved two hundred years apart, one in the Mediterranean and the other at the foot of the Himalayas, they both seem to follow very similar trains of thought.

On the one hand, Stoics consider that happiness is found within one's self and not susceptible or manipulated by factors external to the soul, and Buddhists believe that peace can only come from within if it is to have any value. Their similarities in this basic tenet are striking in the fact that only things that are universally true could be developed independently with the same result.

In Buddhism, the path to Nirvana (enlightenment, for lack of a better word) is to follow a prescribed path. This path encapsulates a set of actions, perception frameworks, and thought processes that one can develop over the course of life to acquire an enlightened state. This path includes the practice of cultivating the right perspective, having the right aspiration, invoking proper speech patterns, engaging in appropriate actions (and disengaging from inappropriate ones), embracing proper living, cultivating deep concentration, and invoking perpetual mindfulness.

If you already have a background in Stoic philosophy, you will realize that most of the elements along this path sound familiar. In Stoic philosophy, the main root that is identical to Buddhism is that the individual is responsible for his own happiness (and, conversely, his own suffering) and, as such, he or she is responsible for the consequences that plague him or her down the road. In other words, if you choose to be happy, you need only to look inside yourself to actions that will consequently lead to the state of happiness you desire. Those consequences are the sum of a number of factors not limited to just the person's actions but also reflective of their perspective and perception, their goals and aspirations, their conversations, righteous living, focus, reflection, and meditation.

The other thing that is almost identical but differs slightly from the Christian-Stoic similarities is that Buddhism does not compel anyone to worship anyone or anything. Followers of the Buddhist way use the statue of Siddhartha Gautama (widely known as Buddha) to remind them of the embodiment of his principles, while Stoics do not necessarily have a personification of their tenets of Stoicism. Many Stoics display busts or portraits of Stoic philosophers in their personal space to remind them of their principles, but those artifacts are not used to worship—only to remind.

That doesn't mean you couldn't have a symbolic reminder of Stoic teachings. A model of the Parthenon is just as good, or the image of Marcus Aurelius would serve the purpose as long as you realize that you are not paying homage to the picture, the bust, or the person. It is merely a way to represent the ideals of the philosophy. Remember the old adage that a picture is worth a thousand words. That's what the picture or statue of Buddha or Marcus Aurelius is supposed to do for you. In one glance, it is designed to bring all the associative thoughts of the principles that bring you happiness and clarity.

The next similarity that plays between the two philosophies is the definition of happiness. Stoicism talks about happiness in almost the same way as Buddhism, and they have similar definitions of happiness as well. That is the key before any further discussion in Stoicism because happiness that is derived from external sources remains at the whim of that source. As such, material happiness comes inherently with self-destruction. The most beautiful flower will wilt, money will erode, palaces will crumble, and gold can one day become worthless. Buddhism and Stoicism do not consider happiness as something that comes from money and possessions but rather as a state that manifests in the wake of practicing and understanding wisdom, courage, and justice. In this respect, happiness in Christianity has a similar meaning. In the Bible, it is said that a rich man entering heaven is like a camel entering the eye of a needle, which is impossible. If you think that heaven is a point in space and a place you go to, then this makes little sense, but if you equate, for academic purposes, that heaven, Nirvana, and enlightenment are the same thing, then you start to see that happiness is a state, and you cannot enter that state while you are distracted by the pitfalls of wealth, the longing for wealth, the disappointment of not obtaining that wealth, or dealing with the consequences of trying to attain wealth immorally.

The next aspect of similarity between Buddhists and Stoics is that they are encouraged to be part of a collective and to contribute to that collective. Whether that collective means you take on some form of public service, whether you take on family responsibilities, or you look after your neighbors doesn't matter, but the essence of the two philosophies promotes the idea of unitary strength. In Stoicism, it is embodied in their propensity to duty.

In the current state of world affairs, happiness has been hijacked, or rather, the definition of happiness has been hijacked in a way that is prevalent and pervasive. We see the idea of happiness limited to the fleeting nature of consumerism and the physical feeling of bliss. There is really nothing wrong with that concept. It is perfectly acceptable for a person to feed the desires of feeling. After all, they are already within us. The confusion and the long-term definition according to Stoicism is that it can get to the point of being a considerable distraction to the efforts and actions that one needs to take to reach that level of peace and happiness.

Departure from Religion

The problem with the typical person's understanding of religion whether they were taught this way or if they were naturally of that mind-set comes from the fact that they were given a set of rules and told to practice it. That leads to all action and no spirit. They go through the motions, doing the rituals without ever understanding what they are doing and what that symbolizes.

Catholics are told to go to church on Sunday, abstain during Lent, go for confession, and receive Holy Communion. Each action and ritual has a purpose designed to evoke a certain internal manifestation. As St. Thomas Aquinas, a philosopher and devout Catholic, articulated in his writings about rituals and inner spirit, external actions are an "outward action of an inward grace."

Religions weave rituals into their practice as a way to evoke manifestations of spirituality from within so that they can come into contact with a higher power. If those actions are just meant to be limited to just the action, however, then that desired spirituality is left out in the cold.

Followers of religions, during prayer, be it Catholics at mass, Hindus at puja, or Muslims at maghrib, are reaching toward a higher purpose. Most do as they have been told and follow the dogma and the rituals without ever understanding the true nature of their actions or where it came from. In time, the spirit of the ritual was forgotten, and only the vacant actions remained, leaving the congregant vacant inside without fulfillment and eventually void of happiness.

The original intent of the teachings in these religions, be it Islam, Christianity, or Hinduism, was to evoke a sense of spirituality, but over time that intent has been lost. If you look carefully at the original words of the founders of the religions or the ancient texts that these religions rest on, you will find that much of what was actually prescribed then is lost today.

With deeper analysis, though, you can see that what they tried to explain does seem to show up in Stoic philosophy, especially when referring to happiness. In Buddhism, they don't look at it in terms of happiness as much as they try to prevent suffering, and they do that by altering their desires and perception just as the Stoics prescribe. In Christianity, they focus on sins of excess, such as gluttony, lust, and greed, and you find that Stoicism as well talks about the pursuit of happiness, which is not found in any of those excesses. Epictetus writes that freedom is not attained by procuring that which is desired but from controlling the desire.

With that in mind, it is also not accurate or equitable to blame the evolution of religion into a vacant set of practices and rituals. A true understanding of theology and spirituality requires time, and most people do not have much of that following a particular lifestyle. They had also lost the plot in most cases not because they were ignorant but rather because they were walking into the proverbial theater in the middle of the third act. The premise of religion failed to pass the intellectual test or the test of logic that a more evolved mind today seeks to understand.

What was missing was any real intellectual philosophy that jived with the logic and reasoning that such people as Socrates and his students had advocated two thousand years ago. Most of the religions and teachings back then did not comport with the powers of reasoning and dialectic debate but instead scratched the surface of observation.

That brings us back to Stoicism today. To dive into Stoicism is to try to understand its intent as well as what people before you have thought and what people after you might think about it.

Rituals

Organized religion is organized because its aim is to get the message out to as many people as possible, and that requires organization. On the other hand, archaic and nonorganized religions were just observations of a higher power and the lack of the human mind to comprehend and be empowered by it. None of it was wrong. It was just who we are and what was available to us at the time.

Take, for instance, the idea of rituals. There were all kinds of rituals in the ancient world—rituals to sacrifice animals and rituals to sacrifice humans—rituals to offer alcohol and rituals to offer food. Other rituals offered words of praise and adulation and burning of candles. All these rituals had a special place in the human psyche and were enhanced with the performance of the ritual that got the participant what he or she desired.

Alexander the Great, the youngest conqueror in history and who swung the Hellenistic philosophies to the east, was a great general and master tactician. But if he were to sit across from you now and you asked what he owed his success to, he would undoubtedly say that it was because of all the rituals he performed before every battle. Alexander would pour libations and offer sacrifices to the gods before every battle, and he would offer thanks at the end of each fight. He is also the only general in history to remain undefeated no matter the odds.

You may wonder whether the gods really hear you when you invoke their help or are they really swayed by your offerings. We may never know the answer to that, but we do know that rituals work, which is why they have been part of every religion in ancient times and today. Even the Catholic Church employs rituals, although they are not called as such. The Hindus in India have numerous rituals as do other lesser-known religions around the world.

We don't really know how they work, but they do. If you believe and perform the ritual, you end up getting what you ask for. In modern-day metaphysics, it is part of the Law of Attraction. Stoics place gravity on rituals, but they do not do so blindly or without the intellectual component attached. They are mindful of the rituals and do not stop at what they know but rather seek greater depth in their practice and their understanding. How does this concern us today in our discussion of Stoicism? It is because rituals have worked since long ago, and we see what works, so we keep doing it. We observed and then we repeated. It also concerns us today because Stoics perform rituals of wisdom. Observation and cogitation became rituals.

Observation

Stoic philosophy has two sides regarding this same effect—observing and then doing. The first is that Stoicism takes observation to a much deeper level. In the early days, Stoics sitting around the Agora used their senses to observe and then brought their observations to a debate and created frameworks to make other hypotheses. Stoicism was, in part, a sort of the derivative and higher level of observation. If you observed the world of rituals, that would be simple observations. It is like having a lucky sock. If you realize that each time you wear that sock you win the game, then you will start wearing that sock every time you play the game. The moment you wore that sock it placed you in a mind-set that caused you to perform better, and what you observed was just really the superficial layer of it.

Stoicism, however, didn't just look at the luck of the sock. It went one step further and started to think about what would connect the dots between the act of wearing that sock and winning the game.

The other side of the coin was logic, which was undoubtedly the vestiges of Socratic teachings. Logic has a bad reputation today. We tend to take the Captain Kirk point of view of this instead of Dr. Spock's. (By the way, Spock was modeled after the quintessential Stoic.)

Some of us think that logic is too dry and not how life was created or how it progresses today, but you may have a wrong and simplistic view of what reasoning and logic are and what they bring to the table when learning about the higher power of the human condition.

We are the leading edge—the latest iteration of billions of years of evolution. (I did say billions because I don't consider the evolution of man to be just over the span of time ranging from the first trilobites; let's consider the evolution of man since the Big Bang). You can't look at life as just the moment when plants and animals came into being for this discussion. That would be incomplete, and that is mostly the reason why it is impossible for non-Stoics to see that we are all part of the same universe.

Stoics see two parts to this equation of life. You can think of all things in this universe as animate or inanimate objects. This is what the Stoics began to understand all those centuries ago. They may not have had insight into the microscopic elements of the human body, but they had reasoned out the nature of living, the elements of life, and the change that is part of everything.

Change according to Stoics is the only constant, and it is that change that you consider to be life. Change signifies and encapsulated the existence of life. Without change, there can be no life.

Even the erosion of solid rock by a stream is an indication of life and nature. It is not the water that erodes the mighty rock but rather the movement. Just as we can see that is not the water that causes the erosion but the movement of water (the element of change), you must also apply the same element of change to see that life exists from that.

The point here is that Stoics distinguish the tangible from the intangible. Tangible covers all the things that you can describe and discern directly from your senses. For example, if you can see it, hold it, touch it, and taste it, that means it is tangible. In fact, if you can ascribe a characteristic to it, that makes it tangible. But these tangible phenomena do not exist in a vacuum. Something holds them together, and that is what we think about as the intangible.

Take, for instance, a car that is stationary. The tangible is the car; on the other hand, the intangible (and this is hard to see at first) is the fact that it is stationary. When the car is moving, however, the tangible is still the car, but the intangible now is its motion. Your eyes do not see movement. You only think they do. It is your mind that "sees" the motion. How does it do that? How does your mind "see" motion?

Your mind sees one picture frame and then compares it to the previous frame. If there is a change in the content, then it detects there is movement. It's like comparing two still shots of a moving car. On one you see the car on the left of the image, and in the second you see it in the center. Your mind then computes the difference, and you realize that the car is in motion. In the days before digital cameras, you needed video to capture frames of images, and then when it is played, the mind sees the illusion of movement.

In the physical world, your eyes see the tangible, but you need your mind to detect the intangible. If you just see the tangible in frames and do not have the mind to discern the intangible, you will be at a disadvantage as to the understanding of all things and their nature. This phenomenon of understanding and of knowledge then develops into the intractable problem in epistemology.

The reason many things in this universe—from metaphysics to spirituality—seem to be the thinking of quacks and folklore is that science demands tangible evidence so that we can all see, feel, touch, hear, and smell as evidentiary proof of a phenomenon's existence, but the most important elements of the universe are intangible.

I can share two examples to highlight this point.

The first would be the existence of something called dark matter. As recently as just two decades ago, science was committed to espousing the notion that space is a void. Scientists said that there was nothing in space, and they confirmed it by saying that it was self-evident. Because they couldn't prove the existence of interstitial matter, they said there was nothing there. We now know that to be totally false. The darkness of space is filled with what we now know to be dark matter. Just because it was not something we could detect with our five senses or any of the instruments that we built to enhance those senses we automatically thought that it wasn't there.

The second example is the existence of black holes in space. We never knew they existed, but

Albert Einstein through inspiration and calculation—and never once visiting space—determined that phenomena existed in space that later came to be known as black holes. He didn't see, touch, feel, or hear any kind of black hole, yet he knew that it would be there. Instead of seeing with his eyes, he "saw" with his mind. Truth requires appreciation by the mind and not by the senses.

The point between the two examples so far is to show that you need to use your mind to see the things that exist beyond what is merely tangible, and it is those things that are intangible that combine with the tangible to make the world what it is. Without observing the intangible, we will not be able to fully understand everything else.

To a Stoic, the philosophy that came about from all the discussions is one that attempts to continuously find the nature and character of things, which gets you closer to seeing the intangible of all things, and when you can see those intangible factors, then you can also see that all things are connected in some way at a very deep level.

As you advance through this book, the point that you should hold in the back of your mind is that the Stoics are in search of the truth. They do this in all situations and in all things, tangible and intangible, animate and inanimate. The truth they seek is not limited to something that one can see or hear, and as such you need to observe with your mind and not just your eyes.

Stoicism is not about a set of rules that get you to see the truth. They don't lead you with rules to the gates of understanding. Stoicism is not dogmatic, and neither are its benefits achieved from actions following rote memory.

It is the revelations that it makes with allegories, principles, teachings, and experiences of other practitioners that prompt you to see things in a way that makes you come to your own epiphany. Stoics are crafted from the powers of their own observation and not hammered into acquiescence from the canons of organized instructions.

It takes time to think and reflect—two essential skills that form the prerequisite of any aspirant of Stoic living and then graduate to seeing the nature of things—the inanimate we discussed earlier. There are no rules; there are only best practices and experiences of men who have climbed so high atop the pinnacle of intellectual truth that we sometimes need a sprinkle of faith to follow in their footsteps; otherwise, we will not be able to understand or see what they see.

There is one other battle that you have to wage if you are indeed interested in seeing the truth, and that is to shed the limitations of your evolved body. Many parts of you are still catching up to what you know today, but it is still part of what you were yesterday. By that, I am referring to the sense of fear that is in all man today. We fear, and thus we are unable to climb. We fear, and thus we are unable to see. We fear, and thus we are left static and immobile.

Being Stoic is by nature to be dynamic in one's understanding. You cannot be stagnant in your quest or your effort but rather to see all there is to see and yet still remain at peace and in a state of calm while pondering and executing each move deliberately and with full knowledge of what happens next. The Buddhists have a simile that describes this, and it is referred to as the Simile of the Raft.

The abridged version of this is that a man roaming the forest comes to a river that would be impossible to swim across. Seeing that he needs to cross, he decides to build a raft from the many logs, branches, and twigs, and the grass that grows on the banks. After some time and considerable effort, he completes a sturdy boat and sets sail across the river. Once he reaches the other side, he is hesitant to leave this boat on the shore and considers carrying it on his back as he proceeds on his way through the forest. On one hand, he is not willing to put in such a magnitude of effort to carry the boat on his back, but on the other hand, he does not wish to leave his hard work behind.

In the pursuit of truth, we often come across many tools that we use to help us gain momentary advantage and to cross raging waters to get to the other side. Once on the other side, we tend to do like this man did. We carry the raft on our backs for miles. At this point, the raft goes from being a tool to being a burden.

There is a process of evolution that we go through as we approach the truth. As long as we continue on this path and leave the old tools behind, we will be free to see each experience without the burden and with appropriate perspective. This is the way to see things as they are.

Chapter 2 - Historical Roots of Stoic Philosophy

"It is high time for thee, to understand that there is somewhat in thee, better and more divine than either thy passions or thy sensual appetites and affections. What is now the object of my mind, is it fear, or suspicion, or lust, or any such thing? To do nothing rashly without some certain end; let that be thy first care. The next, to have no other end than the common good. "

— Meditations, Emperor Marcus Aurelius Antoninus Augustus, 180AD

The Athenian philosopher Socrates remains the titan and anchor of modern Western thinking. His influence spread across Greece and on to the provinces of Rome and then on to the Western world, still referenced and studied intensely today.

It would take volumes to describe and explain all of his teachings and ideas, but three are relevant to the topic of Stoicism and its history. The crux of these three legs strongly advocates the need for self-understanding, and he is widely cited for saying that *"the unexamined life is not worth living."*

The first leg of his teachings strenuously advocates the fact that one needs to discover his/her own purpose and to do it on their own. Most of his teachings were based on the idea that we can find most of our answers within, and reflection and meditation provide the necessary tools to do that.

The second leg of his teachings involves the care of one's soul. In his words, the soul refers to the being beyond the flesh. It is more important than any physical component of the body, and it goes beyond the mere brain. The soul is the intangible within us that we can't see using our senses, but we can detect it if we use our mind. The care of the soul that he talks about, and it can be found in Plato's writings (since Socrates himself never wrote books or pamphlets), are ways in thought and action that do not degrade the existence. Most of this is achieved by refraining from indulgence in excess and not allowing pleasures to dictate actions.

The third and final leg of his teachings touches on the need to act out the goodness of the soul in terms of the way one interacts with others. His whole idea was not to evangelize but rather to exercise. Even in his own teachings he didn't explicitly lay out tenets and rules; instead, he employed a new way of teaching in those days, and it has come to be known as the Socratic method, and that method has become the basis of Stoic inquiry.

This method was simple to break down any observation or unknown into a series of questions. It is also known as the science of argument, or the science of dialogue, and works as the foundation of logic. The logic that we speak about in most conversations has its roots in this, but we don't always refer to it in the same way.

Logic and argument were so intricate to the Stoic pillars that they reformed language and the formula for a conversation to be able to transmit and analyze knowledge.

But this didn't happen in a sequential and urgent way. Socrates was not the founder of Stoicism, but he was the father of the logic and methods that led to its foundation almost a hundred years later.

The Socratic method, which we take for granted today, was not the norm in 400 BC. In fact, even toward the end of his life, the Socratic method had not become a mainstream discipline and only occurred after his passing thanks to his students, especially Plato.

As mentioned earlier, Socrates never wrote books or pamphlets. His main methods of research and the ideas he formulated were not memorialized by notes and texts but by teaching and discussing it with his students at the Agora.

Academy School of Thought

It was his student Plato, who under the auspices of Academy, a school he set up just outside Athens, who had refined Socrates' teachings and wrote about him. This Academy continued to breathe life into the words of Socrates and the concepts and methods he had developed in his lifetime. It also added to the conversation as Plato continued the tradition of exploration and development of the logic, reason, and methods of Socratic dialogue.

Socratic dialogue is an important element of Stoicism, even if it did predate the founding of the Stoa Poikile school by almost a century, and it is important that those who wish to understand the true nature of Stoicism understand the fundamentals or at least the methods by which the reasoning evolved up to that point.

Socratic dialogue is unlike other methods of knowledge distillation and synthesis. In comparison, a debate is heavily reliant on prose, oratory ability, and theatrics to some extent. It takes a short amount of time to get to the conclusion, but it leaves out important points that the lesser orator may have championed. In contrast, elections are inefficient. It has nothing to do with what is right, and worse, nothing to do with what is the truth. It is easier to conduct over a wide swath of participants, and for that reason, it serves its purpose in specific situations.

On the other hand, Socratic dialogue is more about reaching the truth. Socratic dialogue starts with a question, for example, "What is happiness?" From there a group of people get together and ask questions that penetrate deeper as they peel back each layer. Unlike balloting or debating, every question gets answered to the satisfaction of all before moving to the next layer. In this way, the topic is holistically viewed, and no gap is left to fester.

This was the process that led to Stoicism. It was from the Socratic dialogue that resulted in the idea of human existence and the distinction of human knowledge from human assumption. It is what first Plato's School, Academy, which, by the way, is the reason the name Academy applies to an institution of learning today.

However, Plato was not the only one to extend the mind and thoughts of Socrates to the next generation. Socrates just sparked the movement, and it took a hundred years of thought development beginning with his students Plato,

Euclid, Antisthenes, and Xenophon, and then advancing it to their students. From Plato, it passed to Xenocrates and Polemon, both heads of the subsequent iteration of Academy.

Megarians School of Thought

In parallel, while one vain of Socratic philosophy matured along the Academy track, Euclid of Megara, a mathematician, was developing a school of philosophy called the Megara. The Megarians School differed from Plato's Academy in many ways, but stylistically, it was more of a critique of the shortcomings of the other methods of getting to the truth.

A layer above that then it was one that was purely innovative. In the grand scheme of things, that is not a bad thing. It was actually a positive development at the time, and it went on to being a significant contribution to the development of Stoic philosophy, which was still at least eighty years away.

The Megarians brought another important piece of the puzzle to the table. They injected the part about goodness and wisdom. The Megarians contended that this good was an ethical imperative because they saw "good" as ethical and not as just a nicety.

In time they developed the ethical component of Socrates, and as the newer generations entered the Megarians, they introduced paradoxes into the conversation. To be clear, Aristotle and the Megarians clashed intellectually, which allowed the Megarians to further refine their stand, and that turned out to be a positive force in the eventual development of Zeno's Stoa Poikile.

From Euclid the baton passed to Thrasymachus of Corinth, and from him it went on to Stilpo, who progressed in the ethical development of Socratic philosophy in the Euclid's Megarians school. By the time Stilpo was teaching Megarians, it was almost a century since the passing of Socrates, and in that same span of time a third parallel track was being developed.

The Cynic School of Thought

This third track was that of the Cynics. Antisthenes, another student of Socrates, developed his own school of thought and proceeded to spread its teachings that were part of the mainstream before retreating around the time of the rise of Rome and then rising again a century later.

The Cynics are not what you think the word generally means in the English language. The Cynics are not ascetics contrary to some belief. Cynics tend to think that a life of virtue is one that is lived in agreement with nature. It is often mistaken to live in denial or live in exclusion of comforts as a way to punish one's self, but this is not entirely accurate. Cynics immerse their lives in the separation of self and comfort and do it as a way to retain clarity and piety.

One way to think of it is to see it as the life of absolute minimalism, where there are no forms of distractions and no desire to create disappointments. Between the three schools that erupted in the wake of Socrates' teachings, you can start to see that what came next after Zeno was almost the logical progression of what would happen. What, if anything, would minimalism have to do with any of the teachings of Stoicism? The answer is that Stoicism considers the distractions of daily desires and vanities to be something that can derail a person from what he is truly capable of and what he or she could otherwise achieve—true happiness. To be clear, it isn't the cessation of desire that brings the happiness but rather the errors and the emptiness that the fulfillment of these desires results in or the pursuit and lack of gaining release from those desires even after accomplishment.

One of the key elements of Antisthenes that passed on to his successors and even made it all the way to the founding of Stoicism was the notion of the brotherhood of man. The brotherhood of man he believed and espoused was far more important than any nationalistic or racial divide. No man was different based on the color of his skin, his port of origin, or his language.

From Antisthenes, the Cynic line came to Diogenes. For what seemed like excessive simplicity, he came to be known as the mad Socrates.

Diogenes of Sinope

Diogenes took simplicity to a whole new level, believing that not only valuable and possessions were distractions but also were the more intangible acquisitions of vanity, power, prestige, and status. He reached the point where he would roam naked in the streets of Athens or just wearing a simple loincloth and lived in a barrel that was once used to store olive oil.

For food, he would beg in the marketplace, and, when needed, relieve himself by the side of the street. As reprehensible as this may sound, it signifies a man whose mind had no concern for whatever others thought of him. Eventually, his teachings became so popular and prominent that the Cynic school of thought was brought to the mainstream.

He was revered by others even though that reverence didn't bother him, as he viscerally did not include social appreciation or social structure and status as something that was worth inculcating.

When Alexander the Great once visited Athens and heard that Diogenes was close by, he hurried to meet him. When he got there, he found that Diogenes was sunbathing. He went to the Cynic and told him that whatever Diogenes wanted Alexander would grant it to him. Diogenes lifted his head, looked at Alexander, and said that all he wanted was the sunlight that Alexander was blocking at that moment. He was more interested in his dose of nature than anything the king could offer.

Alexander immediately moved away, and Diogenes went back to basking in the sun. Once leaving the market, Alexander commented to his entourage. "If I were not Alexander, I would like to be Diogenes." High praise from a king.

From Diogenes, the Cynic School passed to his student, Crates of Thebes. Crates was a wealthy man, and once he embraced the teachings of the Cynic School, he gave away all his possessions and lived on the streets of Athens along with his wife, who subscribed to his philosophy. He was also well respected in the city and constantly given food and consumables by passers-by. He lived the life dictated by the philosophy he believed in. His popularity resulted in a steady stream of students who wanted to live the life and find the secret to life that Crates seemed to have discovered. One of those men who wanted to understand his teaching was Zeno of Citium (Citium is pronounced "see-Shum").

Zeno of Citium

Zeno, born circa 336 BC, lived near present-day Larnaca in the southwestern part of Cyprus. Back then it was a Greek colony called Kition, an area with significant Semitic influence. Kition, in Latin, is Citium, thus Zeno of Citium. Zeno was the son of a rich merchant who frequently sailed back and forth across the Mediterranean and often stopped in Athens.

As Zeno matured, he was a voracious reader, and each time his father stopped in Athens he would pick up books for Zeno to read. Much of his reading at the time was focused on Plato's *Republic*, Xenophon's *Memorabilia*, and other texts by prominent writers of the time.

Before long, Zeno developed his own ideas and began to write at a young age before eventually joining his father in the family trade, where he would sail and learn the business until he was ready to set out on his own. Once he did, he would stop anytime he could in Athens to join different discussions and find more books to read.

On one of those occasions, he found a bookshop that carried many of the texts that intrigued him and more topics on Socrates, Plato, and even a treatise on Cynics, so he inquired as to where he could learn more. The Athenian bookseller pointed him across the street to Crates, who was sitting by the side of the street and mocking Athenian passers-by for their wealth and ignorance. Zeno was impressed.

Zeno was about thirty years of age at the time and was just a dozen years away from founding the Stoa Poikile. He joined Crates, and along with the teaching of Cynics, he continued to read up on the other veins of philosophy that had originally emanated from Socrates. Most importantly, he also looked at Plato's Academy and Euclid's Megarians.

The point to remember in all this is that Stoicism is the product of a century's worth of debate, discussion, and teaching that included the work product of various schools of thought.

Chapter 3 - Foundation of Stoic Philosophy

The Stoa that Zeno distilled from the amalgamation of Academic, Cynic, and Megarian schools of thought does not completely reflect the Stoicism that exists today, and it doesn't precisely embody the Stoa practiced by some segments of Imperial Rome during the time of Marcus Aurelius. They did, however, form the basis of it, which is why it is important to understand the evolution of Stoa so that the student of Stoicism can monitor the evolution in himself.

The foundations of the early Stoa principles came from various elements of the three schools of thought that flowed from the teachings of Socrates. At the same time, it was molded by disagreements with other schools of thought prevalent in Athens around the same period. These disagreements with other philosophies allowed the early proponents of Stoa to refine their own thoughts and ideas and to synthesize their position by articulating three guiding issues.

The first issue describes what the philosophy would be about. In the case of Stoa, the concept was about the ultimate happiness of man.

The second was about what predicated his ultimate happiness. In other words, what would one have to do to get to this point of being happy.

Finally, the third guiding issue was how the aforementioned happiness could be extended for a meaningful span of time rather than merely being a fleeting and superficial sort of pleasure or joy. In other words, the longevity of the actions and the echoes of its consequence as it meanders through the natural course of things.

By focusing on these three issues, what they uncovered through decades of argument and experiment was that it eventually touched on every aspect of a person's life. It was no longer just about the sensation of joy or the pain of suffering; it started to encroach into areas of thought, values, behavior, practices, and habits.

What the Stoics had come to realize is that the principles they were uncovering and espousing were the core values of what it meant to live a fulfilling life.

There was an alignment of the stars as well as far as the timing of all this was concerned. Athens was in the midst of tough financial conditions, and many impoverished citizens lived in and around the city. They needed hope, and philosophy was the only way they could see themselves marching out of the suffering that vexed their minds. Of all the schools of thought, they seemed to find it most in the teachings of Zeno of Citium.

The Stoic teachings that had been forged in the cauldron of a troubled Athens were accepted well, and they treated Zeno as a public hero, eventually erecting a statue in his honor in the marketplace and paying for his funeral when he died.

Zeno was not just a philosopher. He had spiritual and religious beliefs that were separate from mainstream thinking and beliefs of the day. Not many were teaching the kind of theistic matters that Zeno espoused, but he had the courage to think about them deeply and discuss them openly.

The fragment of his religious thought that made its way into Stoic philosophy (implicitly) was that he considered a monotheistic structure in divinity rather than a polytheistic truism that was the practice of the day. He had the courage to be considered a heretic. This was chiefly unlike anything that the Athenians or Greeks in general were accustomed to.

His twofold belief was that this monotheistic structure that paralleled Stoic philosophy was that of a single God of fatherly love who promoted brotherly spirit. This created something of a stir. In contrast to a polytheistic structure at the time, his alternative talked about one god that was omnipotent, omniprescient, and omnibenevolent.

He went on to say that the gods they worshiped, such as Athena and Poseidon, were mere manifestations of this single omnipotent god. It was revolutionary and started to take hold quietly. It was a philosophy based on something they felt warm about. They were not about to give up the religion of their ancestors, but the philosophy that he was espousing was at least acceptable because he didn't just disparage the current religious order but included it and gave it a larger context.

Besides, philosophy was not an affront to a belief in God in any way. He was lucky they didn't treat him as they did Socrates whom they accused of polluting the minds of youth with talks of an alternative worship structure.

In all, his Stoic beliefs had hues of spirituality without any hint of organized religion. By espousing Antisthenes' idea that all men are equal, without division of race and religion, he adopted a notion that he was a citizen of the world—something that has been lost in the narrative of the modern world we live in.

According to Zeno's reasoning, God was the father, and all men (denoting all humans) were brothers. If so, then the glue that holds us all together is love, not law. Mind you that this happened three hundred before another man from Galilee would preach the same thing to his followers.

But loving one's brother is not enough. It is just as easy to love someone but disrupt their lives from the preponderance of one's own ignorance. A mother may love her daughter, yet give her the wrong advice because she herself lacks the wisdom to know better. A father may steer his son wrong because he has failed to develop his own self-restraint. There are more areas in life than just love, which Zeno understood. That is the reason he brought more of Socrates' ideas into the Stoic school. Chief among them, he drew from Socrates' four areas of temperance, wisdom, courage, and justice.

To mold these four in the cast of Stoicism, he preached that the chief of the four cardinal virtues was wisdom. He believed that without wisdom the other three would fail. Thus, wisdom became the central product of conscious thought. But if wisdom was the core, then what gave rise to wisdom?

This is the obvious question that the students kept hounding Zeno about and he himself struggled to understand. Before long, it became obvious that aside from observation reason was the key element to build wisdom.

From there the Stoics had begun to purse all matters with reason and observation so that they could attain wisdom. To be able to use reason, they realized they had to alter their perception. They had to put their emotions on hold, and they had to pay attention to the details.

This framework pretty much still exists today. It is still widely accepted that Stoics are quiet individuals and fairly wise, although no Stoic will ever claim that he knows everything or that he is smart since he realizes one thing very early in his pursuit of wisdom—that it is difficult to know everything. The best we can hope for is to be part of a work in progress.

Stoic philosophy could not have spontaneously developed without the other schools of thought, which is why it is one of the most comprehensive and far-reaching philosophies to survive to the present day.

Fortunately, the Agora in Athens wasn't just filled with three or four groups. There were many more. Beyond the Cynics and the Academics, there were the Epicureans (the main opposition to Stoicism), Cyrenaics (pleasure seekers), and Peripateticism (Aristotle's school of thought) just to name a few. All of them had an impact on how Zeno and early Stoic thinking developed.

This was the Old Stoa—the Stoic values that were rapidly evolving and rapidly proliferating through the streets of Athens and the outlying city-states across Greece. The Old Stoa then slowed its rapid early evolution to a more gradual and organic pace as it resurfaced with vigor in the late first century BC. The chronological demarcation between the height of Old Stoa and the movement toward Middle Stoa occurred during the time of Chrysippus.

Chrysippus came to Athens from Soli in Cilicia, which is southern Turkey today. He was drawn by the teachings of the Stoic school of thought and studied under Cleanthes of Assos, who was Zeno's successor.

Although Cleanthes was a major force in the development of Old Stoa, his contributions were eclipsed by that of his student Chrysippus, who magnified and revolutionized the soul of Stoa by literarily adding to the teachings the *"pneuma"* of all things.

Pneuma in the context of philosophy refers to the air within us. For those who are students of etymology, you would probably recognize that pneuma has something to do with air in the English language. For instance, pneumatic has to do with mechanisms using compressed air.

In philosophy, pneuma was how the soul came to be described. Because the soul seems to have airlike qualities in its invisibility and amorphousness, the closest one could describe these intangible phenomena was to equate it with air.

According to Chrysippus, pneuma was about the soul within us, and as fate would have it, it turned out that pneuma evolved into being the soul within Stoa. The inclusion of the concept of a soul marked the beginning of the Middle Stoa, which sparked renewed interest and carried it into pre-Imperial Rome.

By this point, Stoic philosophy had come to be a comprehensive school of thought that encompassed nature, belief, character, desires and pleasures, discipline, emotion, and the soul.

Then the story of Stoa went silent. There is not much documentation that reveals the status of Stoic proliferation at this point, but however silent the state of Stoic proliferation was it was just as widespread. By the turn of the epoch, Stoic values had begun to make their way to the outskirts of Greece, and that intersected with the provinces of Rome.

Circa 160 BC, a grammarian by the name of Crates of Mallus (not to be confused with Crates of Thebes mentioned earlier in this book) arrived in Rome. He was planning a short stay but broke his leg and had to extend his stay to convalesce. While there he began sharing his Stoic knowledge, and it seemed well received. If you are wondering what a grammarian has to do with Stoicism or its proliferation, it's understandable. Grammar was not part of linguistic priority in the pre-Greco period. The Stoics were the first to expound the importance of grammar so that language could be better used as a medium of communication. They wanted to deal in truth, and without precision or accuracy in language that would not be possible.

Once Crates of Mallus described his philosophy, it gained traction there but not by any significant degree. It wasn't until Panaetius of Rhodes, the last true Stoic scholar of Middle Stoa, arrived in Rome that Stoicism caught on with vigor. It happened that he was invited to join the Scipionic Circle. From there his influence spread to numerous other literary luminaries of the time in Rome, and that influence sparked a trend that saw his words enter the writings of Roman luminaires.

As a side note to the importance of Stoic principles, this anecdote is in order: The members of this literary circle appreciated the value of Panaetius' contribution to the furtherance of Stoicism in their midst and were voracious students of his instruction. Panaetius spent a large amount of his adult life in Rome before returning to Athens, but while in Rome he wrote a book on the topic duty, which is today one of the core tenets of Stoic philosophy. His writing on duty was then translated by Cicero himself who went on to title it *De Officiis*.

De Officiis became an iconic treatise among the educated and in the Christian church that was to come later. It was such a major piece of work that it was the second book printed by Johannes Guttenberg on his printing press after the Bible.

Roman Republic

Cato the Younger, circa 40 BC, started speaking of Stoa values in a society that was fast developing both in terms of military conquest and democratic institutions. The Romans had a central body to create laws, and these laws governed the formal conduct between the state and its citizens, between the citizens themselves, and for trade and commerce.

What was lacking in codified law was a framework of conduct that was beyond legislation, yet adhered to with the same fervor. This looser framework came to be known as the *mos moiorum*. Translated, it loosely means mores. In essence, the mores of a people dictate behavior and conduct that is acceptable and pervades deeper than laws could. There is no law that says one has to take care of one's parents when they grow old, but mores in many societies typically dictate that looking after them in their old age is a good thing to do, and society functions better. It is a minor example but one that should draw a distinction between legislation and practices.

By the time Cato the Younger was espousing this Greco philosophy on the streets of Rome and in the amphitheaters, Rome was facing a moral dilemma in that their mores were insufficient in advancing its vast empire.

Cato the Younger had a sister, Servile, who was the mistress of Julius Caesar and the mother of Brutus. Cato the Younger certainly had significant clout in Roman politics and philosophy, but his contributions were not just by bloodline and people he knew. He had significant intellect and morals along with a powerful sense of loyalty to the republic.

He saw the virtues of the Stoic philosophy as something that could supplement and buttress the mores of a growing Roman Republic, and he wasn't the only one who thought this way. Others wanted a better Rome, and Cato was definitely a patriot of the state of Rome and the ideals it represented.

Cato despised Julius Caesar and despised what would happen if Caesar disbanded the Senate and become emperor. He fought Caesar and sought to keep Rome in the hands of its people rather than live under a dictator. His thoughts on the matter were fodder and inspiration for such men as Benjamin Franklin and George Washington, who invoked Cato's words during the American Revolution.

The prolific biographer Plutarch tells us in *Life of Cato* that Cato was a genius in his youth and immensely socially conscious. He exhibited a profound understanding of social concerns and realized that a man's life was made worthy by his contribution.

His ideals did not sprout in a vacuum. Many of his ideals had been part of his grandfather's words. His grandfather was Cato the Elder and also an ardent student of Stoic philosophy.

His study of Stoic values directed Cato the Younger to live a modest lifestyle even though he hailed from a wealthy family and was successful in his own endeavors. The idea was not to remain poor but to live modestly.

Cato the Younger understood clearly that distractions are the path to unhappiness and the fruit of desires, materialism, and pleasures of the flesh. Most tenets of Stoic philosophy came naturally to Cato, and so when he started studying Stoicism it resonated within him naturally.

It was here that Stoicism revived to its higher phase, and this was the start of the New Stoicism. Cato's contribution to Stoic values was a ramped-up sense of duty. Just as Chrysippus modeled Stoicism to include a soul, Cato brought out the sense of duty to its purpose.

With Cato's contribution, the Stoic story had come to be a coherent and robust philosophy that appealed to the higher minds of the Roman world. Even though he was not able to prevent the dictatorship of Rome, he did manage to inject the virtues of happiness, the existence of a soul, and the purpose of duty into the Stoic saga that entered the Roman Empire.

Roman Empire

As Rome advanced under the dictatorship of Julius Caesar and then grew under the direction of the emperors after him, Stoicism gained footing and became part of the mainstream. It had a hand in the thoughts, culture, mores, and legislation that grew from the subsequent iterations of Stoic values and the new Stoic framework that began to exhibit a more Roman flavor. Just as religion today is dictated by the culture it spreads across, philosophy and culture behave the same way.

Hence, the Stoic school of thought began to develop a more Roman vein, and most of the readings, thoughts, and guidelines we find today are of Roman flavor since some of the writers who are popular today were Romans.

Many Romans carried the Stoic torch that was first lit by Panaetius and on to Cato the Elder and his grandson, Cato the Younger. From there it carried on unceremoniously and spread across the Roman provinces, but, more importantly, it penetrated the mind of the Roman citizen to a deeper level. It became the philosophy of the illuminated and the ideals of the patriot.

It had become so ingrained in Roman heritage that by the time Constantine had commissioned the collation and creation of the Bible there was a strong Stoic presence within him and the members who were involved in the collation of the Bible. Stoicism indeed had been a driving force of the Romans who stitched together elements of existing religion with elements of Stoic philosophy to come up with a coherent religion that could go on to dominate the minds of Romans.

Once the adoption of Christianity was complete, Emperor Justinian I abolished the teaching of Stoicism in Rome. With Christianity as the state-sponsored religion, it became illegal for philosophers or naturalists to express their ideas of divinity, and Stoicism had to dive underground. Until now.

Chapter 4 - Observing Nature

"All worldly things thou must behold and consider, dividing them into matter, form, and reference, or their proper end."

— **Meditations, Emperor Marcus Aurelius Antoninus Augustus, 180AD**

With its history behind us and an understanding of how Stoic philosophy unfolded, it's now necessary to lay the foundation of the concept of nature as a Stoic sees it. The nature of all things is directly tied to the other veins that run through Stoic virtues and Stoic philosophies, and understanding it will go a long way for understanding Stoicism.

We will explore nature by visualizing it in different ways to see what it is and what it is not.

A powerful way to visualize nature is to observe a symphony in progress. The overall melody produced by the musicians is composed of individual sounds and rhythms layered atop each other and chain-linked in a specific combination.

Each layer of instruments may have its own melody and cadence. For instance, the wind section may be doing one thing, while the brass and strings may be doing something else. The symphony of more than a hundred different instruments coming together creates a deep and rich experience, even if, individually, their notes, tempo, and even volume are all different at any one time. Not all the instruments from percussions to wind and strings are playing the same musical note. Yet, when they come together, the objective is accomplished.

In the same way, the universe is like the symphony. This universe is not one infinitely large phenomena. It is the amalgam of a countless number of singularities that exist individually, just like the symphony. We don't need to look at the various components to understand the whole, but we do need to at least see the whole in a way that allows us to realize that what we see is not all there is. It would be naïve to listen to a recording of a performance and think that just one instrument made the melody.

But it goes further than that regarding the universe.

In addition to the layers that are detectable to our senses, there are layers that are not. Just because you can't see waves of gravity emanating from the earth and holding the moon in its grip does not mean they aren't there.

Just because you can't see atoms and molecules does not mean they aren't there. You know they exist because you've learned in school that particles smaller than what your eyes can detect do exist, but the exact nature of those atoms and molecules are not apparent to us. We don't even know the truth about them. The models that we use are just best guesses and seem to work well under most conditions, so we take them to be adequately true.

For instance, the atomic model that most of us are used to looks like planets orbiting the sun. In reality, they are not like that at all. For one thing, they orbit in a three-dimensional orbit, and the plates orbit in a two-dimensional orbit. The idea is easy to communicate, however, and works in most situations. If you use this model and just use your eyes to see it, you will be deceived and not grasp the truth.

Our senses can only detect one layer—a superficial one. That layer is limited in scope. When you observe something with your eyes, it is only limited to the amount of light that is present, and since light cannot bend, you can only see the side that is facing you. You also can't see the light that is beyond the visual spectrum, so if there are any electromagnetic emanations from the object you are observing, you would not be able to detect them. As such, you are limited to what you see in terms of dimension and frequency, not more. If the object is at a distance, then you are also probably limited by the fact that you can't hear it, can't smell it, and can't touch it. That makes it even more indiscernible.

The only way you can observe it and make sense of it is to cogitate, observe the effects, and postulate its nature using the faculties of your mind. In other words, you need your mind to observe. That is the essence of the Stoic—to observe with the mind.

Sight, sound, smell, touch, and taste. Anything beyond this—any object beyond our visual range—is invisible to us, and sound beyond our audible range is silent to us, and smell that is too minimal for our olfactory sense to detect is nonexistent to us, and any texture too fine for us is rendered indistinguishable.

This is what Einstein meant when he said that "Imagination is more important than knowledge." He was not referring to the fantasy of the mind or the flittering daydreaming that brings us virtual pleasures. He was talking about the mind's ability to see past what it knows by looking deep into the nature of things. This is the man that imagined the existence of black holes and imagined that time changes as one speeds up or slows down. This is the imagination of a Stoic.

A Stoic understands the world around him because he is not limited to observing with only his senses but subjects it to his enquiring mind.

In other words, you see with your mind, not your eyes; you hear with your mind, not your ears; you taste with your mind, not your tongue; you smell with your mind, not your nose; and you feel with your mind, not your touch.

When you do that, as the Stoic does, you get a deeper sense of understanding in all that you come into contact with, and you begin to absorb the event holistically. That allows you to understand the nature of the object or the event.

Stoicism is a philosophy, not a religion. When you look to understand Stoicism, there must be a reason behind it. You are probably in search of its philosophy or its guidance. That's a good place to start, but it is not a good way to proceed. To come in search of it so that it can end on a better path for you is a good motivation, but you can't meaningfully advance if you think that Stoicism is about to give you a set of rules— human algorithms that would magically give you happiness and insight. It won't. However, Stoicism is about practicing the ability to observe and understand nature, and then you will be able to harvest the wisdom that that offers so that you can then execute the duty that you are uniquely designed to accomplish.

In Stoicism, there is no destination, only the journey. The nature of things is not definable by algorithms, formulas, and step-by-step instructions. It is something that your mind has to observe and penetrate. The defining characteristic of a Stoic is that he develops his mind to see the nature and character of objects and events.

The Stoic drills deeper and observes and then absorbs how all things behave and their nature. In the process, the Stoic is made aware of two things: (1) he is a part of all things that are around him and (2) he must go beyond his senses to be able to take advantage of all the powers and all the benefits that he is entitled to.

This is one reason why the Cynics and other schools of thought that also figured this out realized that they were in search of something much more than just the fleeting pleasures of the flesh. From adulation and respect to fine robes and rich food, the Cynics realized that these factors blunted their ability to sharpen their mind and cultivate their wisdom.

The Stoics are well aware of that but seek to balance the extremes of meager living, and even though it is highly unlikely that you will drop everything and resign to live in a barrel like Diogenes the Cynic or on the streets like Zeno of Citium, you should still contemplate the reason others before you have done so. This contemplation shouldn't lead you to the same actions but instead lead you to the outcome they were searching for.

Stoicism is not about an endeavor that seeks external poverty and internal solemnity. Stoics do not wish to embrace asceticism. The Stoic does not blindly enter a state of poverty but does so with a specific goal to sharpen his mind by dulling his base desires.

Coming back to the symphony, when you attempt to deconstruct the melody, the sequence, and the layers, you find that it gives you endless hours of insight into a number of things that you never thought possible. There are the individual instruments, there is the relationship between pairs and groups of instruments, there is the tempo of the instruments, and also the pitch that it rises to or falls toward. Then there is the volume and the undulating loudness and silence of the piece. They are all different dimensions that you find in one piece of music or even in a single movement. Then you take it from there and realize that each sound when represented on its own means little, yet when placed together means so much.

More importantly, with that particular arrangement of sound, when there is the sequence of strings to percussions or the particular sequence of notes, something happens that only you can feel within you. You either feel elation, sadness, happiness, or darkness. There is an interaction between something that comes in a million different dimensions, and then it affects you in a way that is inexplicable.

What you are experiencing at that point is the layer of nature, and that is what you want to see in everything around you, and that is what a Stoic sees when he observes.

When you think about nature, it helps to think about the symphony and how all the individual parts function, and then the overarching result comes about, seemingly all by itself.

A person's character is the same way. There are countless individual traits, habits, ideals, and assumptions that play on their own, resulting in the nature of a person. This is what we call character. After a lifetime of contemplation, meditation, and reflection, a Stoic aligns all his parts until his nature is aligned perfectly toward his duty. At this point, he achieves his fullest measure of happiness.

Chapter 5 - Balancing Distractions in Pursuit of Purpose

"If it be not fitting, do it not. If it be not true, speak it not. Ever maintain thine own purpose and resolution free from all compulsion and necessity."

— **Meditations, Emperor Marcus Aurelius Antoninus Augustus, 180AD**

The human mind and consequently the human condition is one that is constantly trying to find a sense of balance. Think about it this way: if you are famished, you are driven to eat as much as you can. As you proceed to fill up, the desire that you had to eat gradually diminishes until you get to a point where there is no longer any driving desire.

Each step of that driving desire that is fulfilled (by eating) is rewarded by the sense of pleasure that you feel. When you feel that pleasure or results in a desire in the future to feel that pleasure, that is the basis of a habit.

Yes, eating is a habit. It's not a habit in a way that you may think of smoking or waking up and brushing your teeth, but it is a pattern that is developed based on a desire the body gives you, the fulfillment of that desire, and the reward for fulfilling it. Eating, just like smoking, drugs, or anything else that makes you want to do something, is considered a habit.

The sequence is fairly simple. It starts with a desire. You fulfill the requirements of the desire. You are then rewarded, and that reward makes you feel good. That good feeling makes you remember. So, the next time the trigger of hunger is issued, you are compelled to satisfy it and collect the reward. It is the natural mechanism of the body, and it applies to many ways your body gets you to do things.

That part of things is fine, but things start to go awry when you start forcing the pleasure of reward rather than the underlying need. Stoics shun pleasure not because they are boring people but because they do not want to create a habit and do things because their bodies feel like it.

That is what suffering is made from—the inability to satisfy a desire. Stoics find that suffering is a distraction and, as such, they nip the problem in the bud by addressing the issues of desire.

If you apply the proper discipline and understanding, then that wisdom will allow you to fulfill what needs to be done without the need of being a response to a desire.

If you are disciplined and know when to apply it, you will be able to avoid the trappings of desire and pleasure. That would consequently help you control your emotions.

The Human Need for Emotion

There are two sides to human consciousness. One is reasoned and logical, while the other is emotional and seemingly rash. There are just as many benefits to both as there are flaws inherent to each. To be able to understand the rationale behind Stoicism, we need to look at the emotional aspect of our existence so that we can see how it plays with the rational side.

What is emotion? Is it the urge to cry when things go wrong? Is it the feeling that one is overwhelmed with when one is elated or depressed? What are the characteristics of emotions? Are they valid? These are the kinds of things that you should think of when you are trying to understand the meaning of emotions.

Emotions are not feelings. Emotions are the biochemical responses you have to an event. Feelings are what tell your consciousness that an emotion is triggered. When you break down your psyche, you will find that these feelings of emotions can often be distracting.

There are a number of reasons behind the distractions and the obscuration caused by these emotions. For one thing, the core emotion and the feeling that it triggers can be quite strong, and that will automatically take up the mind's processing ability and render other functional thoughts almost incoherent. It's like it would be impossible for you to solve a math problem if you were being taunted by a bear at the same time. Your mind instantly directs its thoughts to the more pressing matter.

Distinguishing Feeling from Emotion

The feeling of fear, apprehension, and anxiety can be extremely distracting, and if you are in the midst of an anxiety attack, you will quickly realize that there is no way for you to be able to cogently and coherently think about anything.

Feelings are the sensations you feel if something is going on within you. They are a little more than just the tactile sensations that you detect when a light breeze grazes you or when drops of rain soak you. This kind of feeling is not about the tactile input that you experience.

Take it one step further. When you are hungry, do you know it, feel it, or notified about it? What is that sensation? Which internal mechanism alerts you of something going on inside you? Think about that. Identify the mechanism within you through introspection and you will find that there are different components to it. To take an extreme example, imagine if you felt a hunger sensation but you were suddenly chased by a rabid dog. Would you still feel that hunger sensation while you were running? Does that mean your body's need for nutrition is diminished or you just stopped feeling it?

When you feel a sensation of admiration, when the hair on the nape of your neck stands in fear, when you feel anxiety, fear, joy, sadness, trust, or even disgust, that sensation is not entirely a natural response. It is learned. It is learned through experience and so is the response to that experience. It's all learned, and it can be unlearned.

Stoics make the effort to look into themselves to understand the connection between a sensation and the way that sensation is felt. It is a process of getting to know one's self. Remember the Roman saying "Conquer yourself and you conquer the world."

When you respond to a certain event, that response is based on a string of subconscious processes all of which are learned and then internalized. The first is the perception of the event. How you perceive that event determines the range of choices you have. A response is still not part of the process, but it will be based on a range of choices that you have in that subset. So, for instance, if you are empathic, you have a certain range of choices to a given event. That same event will have a different set of choices to a sociopath. As an empath, if you see a child crying because it has lost its parents, you may start to feel an intense sense of pain, but the sociopath will not feel a thing.

That frame of existence will then determine how each person responds. A Stoic does not feel bad when he sees a child cry. That doesn't make him a sociopath. A Stoic, instead, gets to his feet and does something about it if he can. If he can't, he moves on without feeling bad about not doing anything. Action is more important than feeling.

That feeling you get or don't get indicates the sensation that results after this string of perception, experience, and foresight of what may happen next. If you stay in the moment, like being in a snapshot of an event, that event in itself is incapable of rendering any particular sensation and thus no discernable feeling.

Staying in the Moment

A powerful way to balance your emotions and rewire your feelings is to remain in the moment and not project forward or regress into history. The Buddhists call it being mindful of the present.

Stoics see the present as the most valuable of all moments in time. In the present, anything is possible; in the past, you have no control; and the future is impossible to control without setting the events of the present into motion.

When a Stoic stays in the moment, he does it for three reasons. The first one is related to the balancing of emotions because in the present the ability to balance an emotion is ideal.

One can't change something in the past, so an emotion can't be countered. In the future, the events can't be altered unless you change the present, so the emotions presuming the future are a waste of time. That leaves us with the emotions triggered by events of the present, and it is very easy to dilute them with actions you can take to address the underlying cause of the emotion and subsequent feeling.

The Stoic equation is clear in this respect. If you stay in the moment, you are able to do whatever is necessary to handle the issue that is causing a negative emotion and thus a negative feeling. What you cannot do is get caught up with the feeling, and then no one is left in the driver's seat to take the necessary action to counter the emotion with a neutralizing action.

Imagine a deer in the headlights. The deer freezes because of the fear of impending doom. The key word here is "impending." It hasn't happened yet. The deer is afraid of something that is about to happen, but the Stoic knows that if energy is diverted to thinking of a solution rather than freezing a better outcome is more likely.

That's the benefit of staying in the moment

The most common feeling is the feeling of fear. One is afraid of what may happen if he or she were to lose their job. They are not afraid that they may have lost their job in the present. You are afraid of what may happen to your children if they don't do well in school, not that they are not doing well now. Our fear is a projection of what (we think) is going to happen in the future. That fear, the emotion, and the feeling are distractions to solving the problem.

Perception

The next factor in the destruction of emotion is the learned responses to the perception of that event. Say, for example, if you perceive someone is going to harm you, you will not wait to begin preparing your defense.

Perceptions are not reality, but they dictate the subsequent reality of what will happen. Stoics do not give perceptions the weight of truth. They consider perceptions frivolous and would rather deal in truth. In the absence of the ability to discern the truth of the matter, they withhold action and response. It is better to do nothing than to react poorly to the wrong perception.

Stoics spend a lifetime in pursuit of observing the truth. Even master negotiators today use these Stoic skills in ascertaining their counterparts' meaning and intentions.

Wrong perceptions lead to poor expectations and unnecessary escalations in the wrong direction, resulting in suboptimal outcomes.

Balancing Expectations

One aspect of Stoic wisdom comes from balancing expectations. Stoics don't walk into a situation with expectations that are counterproductive. Instead, they do all they can to see things the way they are so that the course of events that eventually unfolds is as close to the path that the Stoic has deduced based on fact and reason.

As part of those reason and fact patterns, Stoics realize that they have to work for the best but expect the worst. In all the possible combinations of work and expectation, they have to cover all their bases and work with the facts and endeavor to reach an outcome but expect the worse.

By expecting the worst, they are not blindsided and left like a deer in the headlights when things don't go their way. Expecting the worst also allows them to divert more resources and efforts toward an objective.

Expecting the worst is what gets Stoics off their laurels and their nose to the grindstone. It is the primary reason behind most Stoics winning the day.

Think about Emperor Marcus Aurelius' following words and how they pertain to expectations:

> "Begin the morning by saying to thyself, I shall meet with the busy-body, the ungrateful, arrogant, deceitful, envious, unsocial. All these things happen to them by reason of their ignorance of what is good and evil. But I who have seen the nature of the good that it is beautiful, and of the bad that it is ugly, and the nature of him who does wrong, that it is akin to me, not only of the same blood or seed, but that it participates in the same intelligence and the same portion of the divinity, I can neither be injured by any of them, for no one can fix on me what is

ugly, nor can I be angry with my kinsman, nor hate him, For we are made for co-operation, like feet, like hands, like eyelids, like the rows of the upper and lower teeth. To act against one another then is contrary to nature; and it is acting against one another to be vexed and to turn away."

This paragraph comes from the beginning of Book Two. You can consider it to be the second chapter of his book *Meditations*. If you understand the history of this book, you will know that Marcus Aurelius did not intend for the book to be published. It was a compilation of his thoughts and philosophy.

He was a modern-day Stoic at the time and had written much of his thoughts and observations in a way that he could read it back to himself during those long journeys and times when he needed his own counsel.

There are two things we can learn from this. If we practice the art of journaling, it will allow us to make more effective use of our lessons in life, but that is not the point of this chapter, which is:

To be able to control the way you respond to things requires that you invoke a certain kind of mind-set so that you will not be distracted or create the wrong perception and then go down a path that reduces your ability to get out of negative consequences.

It turns out that because the human mind is so susceptible to perception and perception is so susceptible to experience it creates a seemingly endless loop. Those who are born into a life of hardship perceive things to always be hard. They can't help it. Those who are born into a life of wealth think differently. A wealthy man, born with a silver spoon, defines a bad day very differently from a man who is born into poverty. That perception creates a reinforcing effect.

On the other hand, it is not just about how one sees himself. It's also about how one sees others. If one is raised to believe in a negative perception of people of certain looks, then whenever they see that person there will be some level of trepidation. The perception-consequence-experience link is indelibly linked unless you take the time to break it through contemplation and reflection.

You may wonder if it helps to start the day as Marcus Aurelius suggests by thinking that someone is going to bug you or be off color to you. The reason he advocates this method is so that you prepare yourself and strengthen your perception rather than fall into it.

Stoics study everything in granular detail so that they can understand the nature of everything, including the nature of emotion, perception, habit, and desire. There is widespread understanding of a person's desire, but it is also important to remember that Stoics realize they need to look inside to understand their own emotion and what triggers it so that they can master themselves.

Having these kinds of expectations will eventually affect your perceptions. This results in your ability to control your outcomes, and that creates your bulk of experiences. If you control your expectations and your outcomes are good, then that creates positive reinforcement.

If you expect someone is going to be bad but you are pleasantly surprised that they are good, all is well. That saves you from a poor experience and allows you to have a better perception in the future.

Expectations and Emotions

Tempering emotion will allow you to see things as they are and to live life as it is really intended to be.

This world is built on the principle of equity and consequence. If you drop a ball, regardless of whether it was intentional or accidental, that ball is going to fall to the ground. It will not miraculously float away and not knock over what is beneath it. You can't wish that away, and you cannot prevent it from happening.

Emotion, however, is something that can be controlled and be an obstacle if it's not controlled. Emotions distract you from seeing the real issue and understanding the nature of what you are observing. Stoics see emotion as a barrier against effective understanding.

We have talked about fear being an emotion that is a projection in the future. There is a very specific reason for that. It is part of our defense mechanism to be able to predict what consequence can happen in the future based on what action we undertake.

If that action is detrimental, then we can expect a consequence that is detrimental. At that point, the mind begins to observe associative features. The mind doesn't just notice the action. It notices the consequences of those actions. "If I release a ball, it falls toward the ground." The next time I don't want the ball to fall toward the ground I make sure I do not release it, and if I want the ball to drop to the ground, then I release it. It is a learned sequence of consequence. Until you experience gravity, you won't know if the ball will drop or how quickly it will drop when you release it.

It's also one of the things that Stoics are not afraid of—they are not afraid to make mistakes because they can learn from them. If you didn't know gravity existed, the first time you released something and it fell, you will learn very quickly that something is pulling the object to the ground. You learn from mistakes, and you learn for getting it right. In essence, you learn from doing. Stoics are not just deep thinkers and observers; they are also doers who reflect on every action from which they can learn.

Emotions and expectations block that experience because they raises the ante by giving you a negative feeling in the pit of your stomach when you don't accomplish your objective.

Expectations and Probability in Stoicism

There is an added layer in the human mind that is built on expectations. What if the expectation is that you do not allow that ball you are holding to fall to the ground, and you know if you do not release the ball it won't fall to the ground, so you should be able to control your destiny with that ability to predict consequences.

But a funny thing happens inside the untrained mind, which has to do with probability. Stoics were some of the first philosophers in the later years to start looking at how probability and the mind started to affect the mind's perception of the outcome and how it anticipated the trajectory of events. There is the probability of known possibilities and the probability of unknown possibilities.

All events that have yet to happen are subject to one of many trajectories. You either know what the trajectory will be to account for it, or you realize that there are trajectories that could come from outside your range of projections.

The mind is a powerful calculator, and it will crunch the numbers and put you in one state or another without you even having to do the math. If the subconscious mind has all the necessary information and knows the calculus, it will run the numbers and give you a sense of what the possibilities are.

However, when you can't crunch the numbers because the mind doesn't have the necessary figures, it is designed to err on the side of caution. It looks at two factors. The first is that it looks at the probability of harm or failure, and then it looks at the consequence of failure.

The more adverse the consequence, the lesser appetite the mind has for even low levels or probable failure. If the consequences are minuscule or nonexistent, then the mind computes that it can afford to take on a higher amount of probable risk.

Look at it this way. Let's say you are playing blackjack and playing with fake money. How much will you bet on the cards you have? You could bet the farm and not worry about it because it's fake. You have nothing to lose. What if you have a winning hand with just a 13% chance of losing? Would you still bet the farm? What if you have an average hand and a 60% chance of losing? Would you still bet large?

Stoics understand that the probability of an event is an important factor in what happens, and so they pay close attention to the nature of things because it is the nature of things that allows us to peer into the world of probability and outcome.

The higher the chances of losing, the less you will be inclined to make a significant bet. The mind works in the same way. The more it sees the chances of a failure, the more it backs off in making the bet. Adversity and consequence are evaluated in this fashion. The higher the cost of failure, the lower your tolerance for it becomes. The lower the cost of failure, the more you are willing to take a risk even if that chance of risk is high.

How does this show up in your conscious mind? It shows up with the emotion of fear and anxiety, which will not harm you but will cause your expectations to be unfulfilled. In the Stoic's mind then, the way to destroy that sense of fear and the emotion that is being felt because of it is to abolish expectations.

Putting it Together

Putting it all together, it is easy to see how most Stoics do well in life and not just in monetary terms. They do well in life in the way they approach things and the decisions they make because they have realized the ability to take the risk in a way that can be effectively mitigated, and then they win. Winners are those who know that wealth can only be built when risk is taken.

In essence, you have to alter your risk appetite and bring it down to almost zero. That is what Stoics endeavor to do and in most cases are successful. They reduce their fears of a future event by understanding that event and then altering the actions so that a series of consequences do not alter their trajectory. When you know the nature of things, you face reduced chances of failure.

To alter your risk appetite, you need to alter your emotional profile. Once you can alter your emotions and assign them to the correct areas of your life, then you will find that you are able to apply logic to all that you do, and the outcome and consequences of your actions create a better path forward.

You are not required to abolish your emotions. Emotions serve a critical purpose in your life, but you need to be able to differentiate when it is a useful form or where it is a distraction and then tone it down so that you are able to think clearly and wisely. Stoics do not abolish emotions but rather take their input into advisement.

If you can only be one or the other, then be logical and thoughtful, but if you have the ability to be balanced, then you will find that applying Stoic principles to bona fide emotional tendencies can give you superior outcomes. To do that, Stoics control the vagrancies and excesses of emotions.

The problem with keeping emotions in the picture is that you end up getting used to allowing it to determine your actions. If you could keep your emotions online but keep them in check, then you will find that you have better outcomes.

When you have emotion and logic constantly working, one of the things that can be observed from the outside is that you are silent and pensive. A Stoic is constantly silent so that he or she can divert the necessary resources to balance their logic and emotion.

The destruction of emotion is not the total annihilation of emotion. You need to break it down so that it does not ride roughshod over your conscious logic and subconscious intuition.

Chapter 6 - Practicing Silence

"Be silent for the most part, or, if you speak, say only what is necessary and in a few words. Talk, but rarely, if the occasion calls you, but do not talk of ordinary things—of gladiators or horses races or athletes or of meats or drinks— these are topics that arise everywhere—but above all do not talk about men in blame or compliment or comparison. If you can, turn the conversation of your company by your talk to some fitting subject; but if you should chance to be isolated among strangers, be silent."

— Epictetus

To use our mind to contemplate the observations we make, we need to set the environment in our mind to be as silent and still as possible. It is almost like looking at one's reflection in a pond. If the pond is in chaos and there are ripples ricocheting from the banks, the reflection will not appear with any real clarity, but if you wait and allow the ripples to dissipate, then the reflection will be significantly clearer.

To be able to do this, we need to be able to manage the silence that is required because the simile of the ripples in the pond describes different lives of silence that a Stoic gradually becomes adept with over the course of his practice.

Silence exists on two levels. First, there is mechanical silence that is created by the cessation of mechanical sound, which is what your ears detect and what your voice creates. This exists on a tangible level and can be altered, created, and silenced.

Then there is intangible silence, which is rather different from mechanical silence in many ways. It is not something that you can shatter with sound. Neither is it something that you can put your finger on directly because you can't capture it with any of your five senses. To imagine intangible sound, just imagine reading the text you are reading right now in a way that feels as if you are reading it in your head. It almost seems that you can hear it, but in actual fact, your ears are not playing any part in this. It's all in your mind.

That's intangible sound.

The mechanical and tangible properties of sound are picked up by one specific sense in the human body—the ears. That is then sent to the auditory cortex for processing before being sent to the amygdala to be encoded and referenced.

Intangible sound has no corresponding sensor in the body like the ears. Your ears, nose, eyes, tongue, and skin can't detect it. That is why it is thought of and described as an intangible phenomenon. It is conjured purely in the mind, and it is something that can be voluntary or involuntary.

When it is voluntary, it is like when we read in silence. When it is involuntary, it is the random thoughts that bounce around in our head. Those are the thoughts that we "hear" and are analogized by the ripples in the pond that continuously bounce off each other. We have no direct control over this, and that requires that we have a strategy to silence it and control it to be able to get to a deeper part of ourselves.

The two kinds of silence are connected at a point that is consequential to the discussion of Stoicism and the practice of observation, reflection, contemplation, and meditation. For mechanical silence to exist, it does not mean that we need to stop all sound around us and cover our ears or enter a soundproof room. A deeper intangible silence needs to be at its core. Without that silence, the mechanical silence will fall in failure; in other words, it will not last.

Stoics learn to control their minds and the conscious process to be able to control the ripples in the pond. The reason it can seem rather daunting for the uninitiated to endeavor to silence the mind is that there are three factors at play.

- The mind's insistence to listen and react to any sound in the world around us. (external distractions)

- The mind's chatter of thoughts that keep triggering based on association. (internal distractions)

- The priority of the thoughts that arise, by association, and derails the mind from being in the moment. (matters of priority)

Practicing silence is a way to neutralize all three factors, and it resides in the core of the Stoics' abilities to get to the truth of all matters.

Strategies to Still the Mind

To start the process, it is helpful for a person to make the conscious decision to reduce the chatter in the mind. To do this, the best aspect of silence to control is the aspect of generating more sound pollution by reducing how much is spoken. The less one speaks, the less the mind is triggered into other associated thoughts and corresponding emotions.

If you are going to be doing this for the first time, get away for the day and go someplace where you can't be reached. Turn off your devices and step into a new environment.

Practicing Stoics today do this periodically, where they turn off electronic devices and unplug from the chaos that may seem like nothing but will creep up on you and disturb your peace.

Parks, nature walks, lakes, and such are good candidates to change your environment when you are doing this for the first time. Such environments will arrest all the tangible sounds that you can control. These tangible sounds that you can turn off or walk away from are the first layer in calming the ripples of the mind.

The sounds that we subject ourselves to, from the music we love to the barking of the annoying dog down the street, are all distractions that tug at the fabric of our peace and set our minds off on a tangent from where it needs to be.

When we silence the distractions that we can control, it releases the mind that has been consciously and even to a certain extent subconsciously locked on to and overwhelmed by it. That consequently affects the thoughts triggered by association—the ripples mentioned earlier.

These thoughts, or thought fragments, that are triggered by association are something we can't control directly. We can diminish them by controlling the tangible sounds that trigger them, and when you extract yourself from the chaos, it goes a long way in accomplishing this. Additionally, when you start to focus on the subsequently diminishing levels of sound, you are actively fencing your mind from the sounds that would otherwise cause those ripples to manifest.

This strategy is a significant part of the process and deserves repeated practice, but it doesn't end here. If you recall, there are three sources of distractions in the mind that we are concerned with in this chapter. We just reviewed the first.

The second involves thoughts that the mind generally throws up on its own. You don't have to consciously trigger a thought, but in a disquiet mind, thoughts have the habit of popping up on their own, and those random thoughts then cascade into a series of other associative thoughts.

These are part of what we also call intangible sounds. You can almost hear these thoughts in your head, and you can almost detect the responses as your conscious mind argues, debates, or converses to quell them or jumps in to agree with them.

When you stop the mechanical sounds, you have accomplished a lot to reduce the intangible sounds, but some of these will still be there. It's a point in time that you will reach to seemingly freeze the chaos around you but not necessarily the sounds within you, which you can't control.

That's when it's time to try a trick that will sweep over you with astonishing freshness. Listen to all the sounds that you can't control—e.g., the sounds of the trees rustling, the sound of the occasional car passing by, sounds of people walking. Focus on them one at a time. Train yourself to consciously hunt and target these sounds and then isolate them.

Find the sound that is most obvious in that environment and pay attention to it. Once you identify and hone in on it and have a good hold on that sound, move to the next obvious sound.

Keep working toward the least obvious sound until there is no other sound that is fainter. Once you are able to go lower and lower to the faintest of sounds, what's beyond that is the silence.

If you are not doing this outdoors, you could simulate this exercise by listening to a single symphony and instead of isolating the sounds of nature, you could isolate the sounds of individual instruments. If you are doing the exercise using music, pick one that has no vocals and preferably pick one that is orchestral. In my experience, one of the best pieces to do this is the first movement in Beethoven's Symphony 9.

Once you learn to pay attention to the individual components of the cacophony of sounds that are around you, your mind will automatically realize what each sound is and that they are unique components of the whole rather than just a droning hum in the background. The mind is powerful this way. Once you pay attention to it, they are no longer a blanket of anonymous sounds that you may find challenging to isolate. Paying attention to them changes your interaction with them and allows you to turn them lower (or completely turn them off) one at a time until they all fade away.

By the time you get to the last sound, you realize that it has been a very active process. There is nothing passive about the art of concentrating or the art of excluding distractions.

Once you get to the last sound and pull that down, what you are left with is silence, and because you have approached this gradually, you will find that you will be able to lock onto it. If you keep practicing this, over time you will find that you are able to identify the silence in the most chaotic of places and focusing on that.

If you lose your grip on it, just go back to looking for that last sound that you were focusing on before getting to the silence, and then start to find that silence that you locked onto from there.

That is the strategy for the second of three situations that we talked about earlier in the chapter. The strategy to arrest the third factor in controlling the ripples in one's mind is fairly straightforward and will be easily accomplished if you have already managed to get the last two strategies to work.

It would be a good idea for you to practice getting to this point for two main reasons. The first is that it will allow you to take baby steps to a practice that is rather daunting if you have not done it before or if you have tried and found that it is quite impossible to focus on silence.

Even though we look at it in baby steps, practicing silence is really an art and not a science. It comes with practice.

Finally, we come to the strategy for the third factor that involves reprioritizing your mind-set. This is a longer-term strategy and one that is iterative. It involves the rewiring of your brain and reprioritizing of issues that you deem important but is, in fact, not critical. There are common troves of misconception that lurk around one's brain, and most of it has to do with some form of fear. It is the reason behind the runaway anxiety that people face.

While all this is what we have talked about as intangible sounds and the thoughts that spring from within your mind, these anxious feelings are ones that you can viscerally feel in the pit of your stomach. In some people, it can be mild, while in others it can be violent.

This book is not about methods to control one's anxiety, but it is worth noting that involuntary or irrational anxiety is common and can be a major distraction to those on the path to practice Stoic values.

Stoicism, it is worth remembering, is best practiced by invoking the highest potential of the mind and to approach an almost spiritual state of existence. The core value that Zeno considered among Socratic tenets of virtue was the element of wisdom. You can't just fall into the lap of wisdom. You have to work at it.

You work at attaining wisdom by focusing your mind on tangible and, more importantly, intangible dynamics that propel the visible and discernable tangible events. You do it by subjecting those focused observations to serious contemplation and reflection. That needs a focused mind, and a focused mind is achieved by quelling the chaos and embracing the silence.

The strategies laid out above should get you to that point.

Chapter 7 - The Layers of Contemplation

"Whatever this is that I am, it is flesh and a little spirit and an intelligence. Throw away your books; stop letting yourself be distracted. That is not allowed. Instead, as if you were dying right now, despite your flesh. A mess of blood, pieces of bone, a woven tangle of nerves, veins, arteries. Consider what the spirit is: air, and never the same air, but vomited out and gulped in again every instant. Finally, the intelligence. Think of it this way: You are an old man. Stop allowing your mind to be a slave, to be jerked about by selfish impulses, to kick against fate and the present, and to mistrust the future."

— Meditations, Emperor Marcus Aurelius Antoninus Augustus, 180AD

A Stoic's ability to contemplate and reflect is like a wizard's wand. It is the seat of his strength and power. His wisdom and the virtues that flow from it are found in his ability to contemplate on matters and reflect on them deeply.

While you practice getting to your silent space, you will find that with each new session you will be able to hold that silence even longer than before. As the span of silence gets longer, you are better prepared for deeper contemplation.

You need this silence in the mind because there are strands of thoughts that can be so delicate that a disquieted mind could shatter the thought. Trying to contemplate with a chaotic mind is more frustrating than productive.

Ideally, you will contemplate in alternating fashion. Start with silence, and when the mind has focused, begin contemplation of the areas you wish to think about. If your mind starts to wander and dig up things that aren't related, let it go for a while and see where it takes you. If you feel that it is too far off the beaten path, then go back to a period of silence and come back to the thought again later.

When Stoics contemplate, they are looking for the nature of that which they are observing. Their contemplation is really a series of whys, how's, and so on. That is the basics of contemplation. You can only see the nature of hits with your mind, and that is what contemplation gives you.

If you don't do this, you will find that you don't have a grip on all the answers while you try to think about them. That's because your mind only stores a minimal amount in your conscious brain. When you are distracted, those distractions are taking up space.

The conscious part of the brain has limited space and limited power to process. The bulk of the matter exists in cognitive suspension in the subconscious part of the brain.

When you cogitate on an issue, you will find that you may be able to work on the issue at a conscious level before coming to a halt. This is because the conscious mind and powers of reasoning at this level can only go so far. To go any deeper and analyze better, the Stoic taps his subconscious processes.

To trigger their subconscious process, Stoics use the powers of silence. When one remains silent for ten minutes and keeps all thoughts and sounds at bay, it is easier for the subconscious mind to move answers to the conscious part of the brain.

When you silence your mind and contemplate a question, you will find that you now have additional answers that you didn't have earlier. This is the most important reason you practice silence even when you are not contemplating anything.

Contemplation

Contemplation is the way the mind digests the subject. This contrasts with observing, which is the way the senses capture the object.

The purpose of the earlier exercise of moving your focus to the sounds in order of descending volume is to train you among other things to be able to focus on what you choose. If you don't gain control over where your focus goes, you will always be at the mercy of external events and distractions.

The next level contemplation is to use reason, logic, and conscious effort to work out possibilities in your head. Until now you have only engaged in conscious processes in your head. One can do that for simple matters but will find it impossible to gain any real benefit in complex situations.

Reasoning and debating can get you part of the way to where you need to be to make a decision or to know the true path that you should follow, but it doesn't take you all the way.

Stoics, however, go one step further. The next stage of contemplation that Stoics engage in happens at a subconscious level. The conscious mind is ideally suited to make observations but not suited to decipher the nature of complex phenomenon.

One of the greatest warriors and generals of all time was the young king of Macedon in the early part of 300 BC. He eventually conquered the largest kingdom in the world at the time—the Persian Kingdom—and was crowned Alexander the Great. At the time of his battles, young Alexander was in his early to mid-twenties— rather young and rather successful without the benefit of mature thinking molded by experiences.

Within a short span of time after leaving Greece on his conquest of Asia, he was able to rule a large part of the known civilized world and a pretty sizeable area of uncivilized tribes to become one of the richest and most powerful men in history. The deciding battle in his victory over the Persians that set this path was fought in modern-day Kurdistan. If it sounds like any other battle in ancient times, it's not. The battle was decisively won, and it splintered the alliances of the Achaemenid Empire. What was amazing, however, was that the Achaemenid Empire came to the battle with a million soldiers. Alexander showed up with fewer than 50,000 men, a ratio of 1:20.

When the battle was done, Alexander had lost less than 1,000 men. His battle plans had been flawless, and his soldiers had executed them brilliantly. How does this relate to contemplation?

Alexander met with his generals the day before the battle and listened intently to their suggestions and plans. The odds, according to the generals, were overwhelmingly against them.

They had all told him that engaging the Persian army would be suicide. Spies had ridden out and scouted the size of the army and reported back with their count. The generals and captains were more than uncomfortable and predicted total loss if the battle proceeded.

Alexander, however, was undaunted. He told them to get ready, eat well, and prepare for the following morning. He then went into his tent and sat down alone. While his generals and soldiers stayed in camp, Alexander sat contemplating for hours in silence. Then he went to sleep.

The following morning the troops were supposed to move out early and enter the battlefield, but the generals had not seen any sign of Alexander. When General Parmenion couldn't find the king anywhere, he went to his tent and shouted many times for him until he finally emerged. The king had overslept.

Parmenion was surprised and asked him how he could sleep, much less oversleep, on the day of the most important battle of his life. In response, Alexander told him to relax and that the battle had already been won. What remained was that they just had to show up for the fight. Alexander had used the power of his mind to play the whole battle in his mind and already knew the outcome.

Historians and priests have long debated his divine inspiration on the eve of the battle. What had happened was that he had gone into a deep state of contemplation, and at the end of it he had found the nature of the event and his strategy and knew what to do.

When General Parmenion came to his tent that morning, Alexander briefed him, and it was carried out. They vanquished an army twenty times their size. That is the true power of contemplation, and it is what defines the power of the Stoic mind.

The main driver of efficiencies that Stoics are famous for is found in that subconscious area of their minds. That area holds the bulk of the processing power and thus the answers to many of their questions. This is part of the reason they never languish in indecision. Doing so is a common symptom of those who have competing perspectives, competing values, or competing desires tugging at them internally. When you straighten these things out, process them effectively, and align them, you find that clarity ensues.

Reflection vs. Contemplation

There is a simple difference between reflection and contemplation. You need to do both, but you need to be clear about the nature of each one. Reflection is the ability to replay the events from the past in your head and look at them individually and find common areas of concern. It is a teaching and self-learning tool. It is not easy for your conscious mind to understand why you do a lot of things, and it is not easy for you to understand some of your motivations for doing what you do. Reflection helps you to observe your own actions and trace a path back to the motivations that result in those actions.

Stoics are very efficient and effective people. They are efficient in the things they do and the issues they think about. They use all that is available to them, even the deeper abilities of the mind.

Stoics value this clarity, and it is the easiest path to identify the truth when it appears and appreciate it. Reflection and contemplation allow you to build yourself to a point that allows you to remain clear of distractions and aligned in purpose. If nothing else, these are the goals and objectives that you should aim for in your quest to understand Stoicism.

To draw the distinction between reflection and contemplation is to be able to see that while they cover most of the same areas you need both to be able to take advantage of the other.

You need reflection to be able to enhance your contemplation powers, and you need contemplation to be able to bring benefit to your reflection. When you fine-tune both of them, you find that the result is exponentially beneficial.

Chapter 8 - A Stoic's Meditation

Imagine a clear glass of water. If you were to place a drop of yellow pigment in it, imagine what would happen. That yellow dye would permeate and diffuse through the water. Even if you don't stir it or shake the glass, as time passed, the dye would diffuse gradually until it occupied the entire space of water. Would it jump out of the water and occupy the air above it? No. Its universe would be the confines of the water, and it would not be able to exit its universe.

Extending that same imagery, you can see that the form of that dye—that cloudy appearance of yellow permeating that water—is suspended in a medium. Without that medium, the dye would not manifest in that same way. That die owes its form to the medium that holds it.

In the same way, the mind, like that yellow pigment, is predicated on a medium. When you need to access the mind's higher level functions, you can't do it in the same way you involve conscious functions. You have to do it by accessing the silent part of your mind—the medium in which the mind floats.

The challenge most people have is to focus on that silence. Because the mind is active and its job is to throw up thoughts and concerns, you find that it is constantly making some sort of observation or alerting you to some possible thought. You have to extract yourself from paying attention to it when you need to, and then the mind will start to tune down.

Think of your total mind as an echo chamber except in this case it's perpetual, and you can stop it until you curtail at least one side of the equation.

Without going into the workings of the mind too deeply, imagine blasting an echo chamber with a sound. What would happen? The chamber will bounce the sound back at you. What if you put another echo chamber across from it? The sound would echo again. It does this a couple of times and then dies down as the energy in the sound wave diminishes much like the ripple in a bucket that bounces back and forth until the energy of the ripple diminishes. Then it goes back to being calm again. That only works when the original echo chamber is passive.

In the case of your mind, it is not passive. Your mind works on the principles of association. If you say one word, it will automatically (and almost magically) respond with another word, and that word will trigger another word, and that will trigger another. So if you were to play the word association game, you will see that the mind is an endless source of seemingly random thoughts or fragments of thoughts.

It is anything but random.

The Mind and Intangibility

The world is composed of two phenomena. The first is tangible—having, for example, shape, size, and mass. A shoe is an object, just like an apple or a car. These are tangible factors.

The second phenomenon is intangible. For instance, whether the car is moving or stationary are intangible qualities. A good way to think about it is to wonder if you can take a picture of it. If you can, it's tangible. If you have to resort to a video recording of it to show the changes it makes, then that is very likely intangible. In this case, movement and acceleration are all intangible properties. A larva's metamorphosis into a butterfly is intangible, but the butterfly and the larva are both tangible.

With respect to these kinds of tangible and intangible properties, it is the mind that can decipher them, which has to be done through contemplation. The brain creates memories of the result and stores it as part of the neural record. The mind is the only tool in a person's arsenal that can convert intangible phenomena into tangible representations in the form of neurons.

The mind has a stage that is built within it, and on that stage it places representations of the various experiences and objects it comes in contact with. Without that representation in the mind, the objects that appear in the physical reality will seem unreal to us. On the other hand, if we have something in our mind but it is missing in the real world, we tend to overlook it at times or feel uncomfortable.

Take, for instance, your home. You are completely familiar with it, and your mind has every detail of the physical space replicated and represented on this stage that it built in the mind.

When you enter this place, the mind is totally at ease with the surroundings because it's exactly as it should be. The observation the mind receives and the neurological imprint the brain has in store are identical. In fact, if the mind is not aware of an alteration in the physical world, it may even neglect to look at its surroundings carefully and might miss something that may have been moved.

Alternatively, think about the first time you went to a certain place. Do you recall the feeling you had in that strange place? It's a heightened state that will have you alert and observant. The more and more you visit that location after that, the more relaxed you start to feel, and you are no longer as alert or as observant as before.

In fact, you may even take things for granted after some time. You could even close your eyes and know exactly where everything is because of that neurological imprint of your environment.

The mind is not looking at your physical surroundings and making decisions directly. It is making decisions on that virtual stage built in your mind. That works for both tangible and intangible phenomena.

Here is one way you can visualize that. If you've played tennis, you would realize that the ball is too fast for the eye to catch and respond. In fact, your mind only anticipates its location based on what it sees your opponent doing and the kind of court you are playing on. It calculates from there and allows you to react. If it gets it right, then it reaffirms the calculation it uses. If it gets it wrong, then it updates the calculations. That's why the more you practice, the better you become.

How does meditation come into this?

It comes back to your physical mind. Remember that your memories are made of neurons, and each neuron is connected to other neurons by axons. Each neuron can have numerous connections—dozens, hundreds, or thousands. When you play the word association game, one word will trigger another because they have this connection between their respective neurons.

It turns out that these connections are not fixed. They can be altered, and the neurons can be moved around. This is called neuroplasticity, and it specifically refers to the alteration of the layout of the neurons and the ability of the brain to alter what neurons connect to, which, in turn, results in thinking patterns that can be altered.

If someone has a poor mind-set in that they constantly think of bad outcomes and they associate negatively, then anytime they hear a certain trigger word or phrase or are exposed to almost anything, it will fire up a range of neurons that are destructive in nature.

This comes down to a simple issue of just poor associative connections, and they can be altered by reconnecting the neurons through a process called neuroplasticity. Stoics in 300 BC didn't know anything about scientific neuroplasticity, but they did understand the power of reconditioning the mind to improve the decision-making process. That, in turn, improves outcomes.

That brings us back to perception, reflection, and contemplation. When you understand reflection and contemplation, you are forced to deal with issues with the same groups of neurons firing whenever you approach a certain issue— just as you may constantly be shouting the word "shoe" each time you play the word association game when someone else shouts "brown." Somehow in your neurological set the word "brown" is related to a brown shoe, so you respond by saying "shoe" when they say "brown."

You're not going to always pick "shoe" because on different days the choice of the responses may jump the neurons from one step to the next or down two steps or even ten steps. The universe of possible responses is fixed by what your neurons are connected to. It can be any number of responses, but those responses can only work if they are connected. If you have "cucumber" on a different set of neuron connection, the utterance of "brown" is never going to evoke your mind to respond with "cucumber."

Think of your different neuron sets as a multiverse of possible neuron bunches. It's easier to think of them in binary terms about whether or not each bunch is connected. In reality, it comes down to how many connections exist in the brain. All bunches are connected with at least one connection. If they are not connected, the probability of getting to that memory drops to exactly zero. If you want the simple explanation, then just think of them in the multiverse. The higher the number of connections emanating from a neuron, the greater the chance that that neuron will be invoked.

If you look at an MRI of a brain during its regular activity, you will see flashes of energy around areas of activity. These flashes seem random but are not. They gravitate in waves of associated neurons. When these neurons fire, they trigger the neurons they are connected to, which means that when you have an idea or are subjected to a specific event, you will always have the same associative thought that triggers in its wake.

The only way to change that is through cognitive conditioning and neuroplasticity. This is where meditation applies. When you meditate, the neurons are moved around and aligned in a more efficient arrangement. What you find is that one event triggers a different set of thoughts and responses than it did before the relocation of the neuron. The more you meditate, reflect, and contemplate, these neurons arrange themselves in a better formation, and you are destined to have better cognitive outcomes.

The Stoics during Zeno's time did not come close to knowing the neuroplasticity effects of meditation. What they did know was that there were positive effects from it. It altered the way they thought, and when the altered thinking sequence yielded better outcomes, the positive reinforcement solidified the change.

That is the whole idea of a Stoic's meditation.

Chapter 9 - Anger and Stoicism

"Keep this thought handy when you feel a fit of rage coming on—it isn't manly to be enraged. Rather, gentleness and civility are more human, and therefore manlier. A real man doesn't give way to anger and discontent, and such a person has strength, courage, and endurance—unlike the angry and complaining. The nearer a man comes to a calm mind, the closer he is to strength."

— *Meditations, Emperor Marcus Aurelius Antoninus Augustus, 180AD*

Stoics approach the topic of anger with the primary purpose of understanding its deeper roots and motivations. The eventual understanding of anger that results from this approach then leads to the ability to limit its force in the Stoic's thought pattern and annihilate its effects across other psychological and physiological areas.

Anger in whichever form, however intense, and under whatever condition is a distraction to rational thought and thus an obstacle to a Stoic's desired state of mind.

Anger is a term that applies to a wide range of states, ranging from mild irritation at the low end of the spectrum to a fly-off-the-handle rage that exists at the far end. The state of anger at any degree does not exist in a vacuum nor can it be spontaneously created or extinguished. However, it almost always seems to the person that endures it as though it comes from nowhere and leaves a swath of destruction in its path before suddenly disappearing. It's no wonder that Stoics call it a temporary state of madness.

Just as a hurricane that seemingly comes from nowhere wields destruction in its path and then vanishes after an inexplicable intervening event can be studied and understood so, too, can anger. It, too, seemingly swells from nowhere, destroys things in our path, and then quells after some intervening event be it time or our better angels. The similarities don't seem to end there.

Just as the hurricane has causes that we can't see with the naked eye, anger's causes are not easily detected by our consciousness, and that is why we think that it comes from nowhere. This fallacy is the main reason those with anger problems and those who only experience anger occasionally think they do not have the wherewithal to control anger.

Anger, in its original design, is about regulating the response to a particular situation a person is faced with, but anger is not a simple emotion. It is not just one faculty of the mind, such as fear or hunger. Anger is a complex state that is the amalgamation of various faculties in the mind.

By understanding the genesis of anger and seeing how a Stoic overcomes it, we draw benefit from two areas: (1) we can use the same strategies to our own bouts of anger, and (2) we are able to understand the mind-set, philosophy, and nature of a Stoic.

Stoics are nothing if they are not master observers. To be able to observe, they invoke more than their senses. The invoke their mind and the powers of reason, and when they do this they start to take notice of the genesis of anger and the similarities of the causes and reasons behind each path that leads a person to that point of rage, irritation, or even frustration.

Stoics see anger as the attribute of a weak mind, which is easily swayed and inherently unstable. Instability is marked by the ease at which it can transition from a stable state to a state of chaos. In essence, a weak mind is one that can be knocked of its perch with the gentlest of breezes.

When you interact with a Stoic, there is almost nothing you can say or do that will destabilize them. Not only have they mastered the ability to not get angry, but they have also gone a few steps further. They have mastered their own mind to the point that it is not easily knocked off its perch.

The reason why anger is a good place to observe a Stoic's ability is because it is the easiest to fall into, the hardest to spot, and the most vexing of complex emotions. Once you have an understanding of how a Stoic manages anger, you can apply the same approach to many of your other situations.

When discussing anger, there are three stages of interest:

- The first stage refers to the elements that trigger the anger. These triggers are generally external (but could be internal as well) to the person and their mind. It is the point at which the person begins the process of cascading toward irrational behavior (anger).

- The second refers to the path that you start to traverse once the trigger has been initiated. It could start with getting cut off at the checkout counter, then someone cuts you off at the light on the way home, then someone jumps ahead and takes your parking spot. It's just a series of events that individually would not have been so much of an issue except that the original trigger set you on a course toward anger. We know this well and often refer to someone "going postal."

- The final stage is the manner in which that anger is expressed.

Stoics break down the complexity of anger by looking at its manifestation and, more importantly, the triggers that become full blown. Anger does not surface in a vacuous environment. It always has a cause whether that cause is real or an emotional response to a perceived event.

This allows Stoics to gain power over anger because both aspects of that understanding, i.e., that it is an emotional response and based on perception, are within one's field of influence. Who among you can say that you can't control your perception? Or, who among you can say that you can't control your response? You can.

You can control your perception, or you can control how you respond to the situation that results from that perception if you just pay attention to the moment. This is the reason why being in the moment and staying grounded in present reality is a key Stoic requirement.

Typically, we only control the outward action of a response to things that happen to us. So when someone cuts us off at the checkout counter, the irritation wells up inside, but the outward action is one of calm. This is especially so when we have to force ourselves to hold back our responses.

Stoics find this inefficient. So much energy goes into creating the original response and then more energy to hold it back. Instead, Stoics learned that if they could just alter the way they perceive incoming stimuli and alter those from being triggers, then they would not have to expend the energy to hold themselves back.

The Distortion of Anger

Putting aside the effect of anger on those around the aggressor, there is the matter of anger distorting present and future perceptions. This is equally detrimental to the person getting angry and the person facing his wrath.

To the person in the midst of an outburst, there is a situation that persists from the time the trigger is released and extends for a long time after the anger and the event in which it existed has passed. This is because the moment the trigger has been released the percolating anger begins to disrupt the person's perception, and everything that happens after that point is tainted. This is the first element of anger that is unacceptable to the Stoic.

The problem with distorted perception is that the information stored in one's memory during the outburst is not filtered or adjusted for that anger. It is stored as is, and that memory that is encoded is encoded with the element of anger that does two things—both detrimental to future issues. The first is that it taints that particular matter that was in discussion, and second it reinforces the state of anger because it is now associated with that event. The more anger outbursts a person has, the easier it becomes to walk the path toward a full-blown incident.

This distorts reality for the person who experiences anger.

The second distortion happens within the victim's psyche. The person that anger is directed to gets an avalanche of negative energy, and whatever is being communicated to them is not making sense because the angry person is incoherent and unreasonable.

Anger distorts the present and sets up the foundation of a distorted future. Anger gets baked into the mind-set of individual situations. As such, when a similar situation is triggered in the future, it triggers the feelings that were aroused in the face of anger, and that is unpleasant, distracting, and counterproductive. Anger is negative reinforcement and may be a short-term solution, but it is catastrophic in the long term.

Not only do Stoics choose to temper anger, they also choose to stay away from those who practice anger.

Chapter 10 - Stoic Minimalism

"Contentment comes not so much from great wealth as from few wants"

— Epictetus

Some of the things that the ancient Stoic philosophers did may shock you if you were to read accounts of their daily practices, but you have to move past the obvious impressions and take a step into the minds of these men. Socrates himself had a home and aids to assist with his endeavors, but some philosophers who developed Stoicism, such as Crates, Diogenes (not a Stoic but contributed to it), and Zeno, chose to live on the street without any possessions or security.

Take Diogenes, for instance. As you've read, he lived in a used olive oil barrel on the outskirts of the Athenian marketplace and panhandled for food. His time was spent thinking of life and higher pursuits. Think of all the threads that entails. No home means no shelter, no place to put food, or keep it clean. No washroom facilities and no moments of privacy. The list of what you don't have when you don't have a home and live on the street is endless. Not many would be able to do that today.

Not having a home means you have no need to spend time maintaining it, no need to earn to pay for it, no need to worry about what is going to happen to it, and no need to spend time on all the things that go into it. All that time you don't spend on a home results in time that you can put toward reasoning, cogitating, and seeing clearly without fear, favor, or frustration.

However, since this is not a book on asceticism, we don't want to advocate the complete abolition of possession. However, we look at it to make a simple point that the more you take out the need for material goods, the higher levels of contemplation your mind can reach.

This was primarily the reason Crates, Diogenes, and the hardcore philosophers of that time sought that kind of mental state to raise their thinking. There are certain areas in India and Vietnam where certain sects of Hindus and

Buddhists spend days panhandling for food near the temple to alter their perspective. Even though they know that after a day or more they will return to the comfort of their home and the food in their kitchen, the panhandling experience alters their minds in a way that allows them to think at a level of clarity that you just can't achieve with creature comforts of the modern home.

All this is nowhere close to what we need to accomplish in our efforts to embrace or practice Stoic virtues. We do, however, need to move in that direction to a certain degree. To put it in context, take a look at the life of someone such as Warren Buffet. Taking his life as an example makes a lot of sense, especially when you see that he is the third wealthiest person in the world behind Jeff Bezos and Bill Gates.

He still lives in a mediocre house and drives a used car—the same used car he drives to the airport to pick up his good friend Bill Gates. He lives an earthly and wholesome life that is so far in the background that it doesn't bother or distract him. There are others like him. Take

Kristen Bell, who showed up at the Oscars wearing a dress that cost less than $50; or Leonardo DiCaprio, who drives a Toyota Prius. These are people who make millions a year and regardless of whether or not they give to charity, the point is that they do not allow the trappings of wealth to blunt their mind, tarnish their soul, or alter their other gifts—and for this they get better at what they do and increase the quality and quantity of what they contribute.

Stoicism takes that path to minimalizing distractions a step further. In the same way, we made the point that religion is like processed food and Stoic philosophy is like whole food. The point is that you need to take time to understand and feel the wisdom for yourself.

The cornerstone of Stoicism is wisdom, but to get that wisdom is not about how much you read. It's about how much you contemplate. When you take philosophies and use them as guidelines, they become dogma and pretty soon are indistinguishable from religions and laws that tell you what you can and can't do without ever knowing the reason why.

Take, for instance, this topic of Stoicism. To really understand and benefit from it, you should equip yourself with the knowledge that is available, but that is not the end of it. It can't be sufficient because what we read and hear can never communicate all that is required to reach a state of happiness and accomplishment. What we need is the contemplation that happens in the midst of acquiring this knowledge.

To put it simply, reading gives you knowledge. Experience gives you insight. Contemplation of that knowledge and insight gives you wisdom. To be able to get that wisdom, you can't be constantly distracted and aloof. That's where minimalism is important. People such as Diogenes shunned all possessions, including the materials that one needs to live on a day-to-day basis. He also gave up on accolades and matters of pride, such as adulation and the need for respect from others. In this respect, when he was called a dog because he was out roaming the streets almost naked and eating trash or what was given to him, he responds with glee, saying that a dog has a heightened sense of awareness, always living in the moment and not having the anxiety of what comes next.

In today's context, that kind of behavior is rather extreme and most likely inappropriate, but hearing the story in its raw form can do one of two things in you. It could either invoke a feeling of disgust and judgment, or it could cause you to stop and think about what Diogenes was trying to say and why so many people shun the world of material goods even if they have made a tremendous amount of money.

There are two points that are being presented: (1) the direct issue of distraction and (2) the importance of contemplation.

As for the first point, the richer you are, the greater the possibility of and propensity for distraction. That distraction is not just about what you can do with your wealth. It is also about how you see yourself and the fact that you think you have already made it. Stoicism sees the opportunity to be minimalist as a way to avoid factors that would otherwise cause you to spend time away from contemplating tangible and intangible events. To be able to understand the soul (the pneuma) of things, you have to see it with your mind and can't be distracted.

Today, it is not possible for you to live on the streets and contemplate the state of life or the pneuma of anything at the same time. It was all right for those men in Athens, where it didn't get too cold at night, or if it did there was always a way to get warm. But you can't do that in Buffalo, New York, in the middle of winter. Having a home today is a necessity to keep you protected from the elements.

The Aristotelian principle that eventually made its way into Stoic teachings was insistence that balance was more important than extremes, and many Stoic teachers in the Late Stoa did eventually realize that the extreme did detract from the objective more than they contributed.

That brings us back to the happy medium—the Aristotelian Golden Mean, which never officially made it into the writings of the Stoics, but they did eventually see its benefit. The Golden Mean does not advocate minimalism, but it does advocate balance between extremes.

How does the balance of extremes come about to being minimalist, since minimalism sounds like an extreme in and of itself? Minimalism is not an extreme situation. In fact, the moniker itself is misleading. Putting the notion of the name aside, lets reassociate the name to what it really is and not what it seems to indicate.

On the one hand, you have absolutely nothing. No clothes, no home, certainly no vehicles, and no prospect of a future meal or any kind of comfort—literally the life of a dog, as Diogenes relished in. That is the extreme end of the spectrum, and that is the life of an ascetic. On the other end, there is an absolute and indulgent luxury. Not only do you have everything you need for today, but you also have everything you need for three lifetimes—that's the quantitative dimension of excess.

Not only can your cell phone make a call, but it can also also drive a car. Not only can your house give you safety from the elements, but it can also house an entire army. Forgive the exaggeration. The point is that luxury denotes a two-dimensional state. Not only do you have more than you need (quantitative) (e.g., the number of rooms in your house, but you also have it painted in gold (which has no practical purpose). That's qualitative.

Minimalism seeks to blunt both edges of that sword. It seeks to occupy the mental space where you don't need to subject yourself to an ascetic lifestyle, and you don't need the quantitative or qualitative aspects of excess. You straddle the middle.

It is rather tricky to find where the center of mass is in this equation. If you don't want to be naked like an ascetic and dress in golden threads like Midas, then what is the center of those extremes?

The answer is simple, which is the first point of minimalism. You have to contemplate. Getting a list of things that you should throw out or steps you should take to get yourself to be a minimalist is not the best way to be successful. Remember that Stoicism is not about following steps or completing lists. It is about contemplation. Only when you contemplate will you be able to find wisdom.

Once you get to that point, you should ask yourself if that is the minimalism that you envision, or are you now richer than you expected? The answer to that is pretty shocking for most people.

Once you shun the excess because those excesses are going to be more of a distraction, then what you find is a life that is uncomplicated and uncluttered. That reduction of clutter has many therapeutic effects, but that is not the reason you set a course on understanding minimalism. You chart this course to minimalism as a twofold exercise. The first is to mold your mind into contemplation, while the second is to understand the nature of contemplation.

Let's look at another example. They are not directly related to minimalism in the common sense of the word, but they are alerted to the way the human psyche approaches them and the faculties of the mind that are involved in both those areas.

For this, take a look at fasting. What do you suppose are the general reasons for fasting? The most common one is to lose weight or be healthy. When is that the rationale behind fasting? Someone who is in good health with an ideal weight (or even a little under the ideal weight) would not consider fasting, but fasting is not just about the food aspect of it. Fasting is about the resilience of the mind. To be able to stop something that is perceived to be imperative to survival makes the mind stronger. By fasting, you shift the power balance between the body's request and the mind's resolution.

This is the higher purpose of fasting. In the same way, there is a higher purpose for minimalism. When you contemplate the nature of being minimalist, you will first learn that you are merely getting yourself back to basics. Why buy a car that has twelve wheels when you can just as easily get to work in a car that has four (or even three)? Why take a car at all when you can get an Uber? But it goes beyond that as well, and when you peel back the next layer of minimalism, what you find is that the human mind is built to take things to the next level. That even applies to excesses. Today, you buy a car that unceremoniously takes you from Point A to

Point B. Tomorrow, you want that car to have a stereo in it; the day after you want it to be able to travel rocky terrain (even though you don't necessarily do that); the next day you want it to be able to have all kinds of gadgets and gizmos and consume a gallon of fuel for every 3 miles that you drive. We tend to snowball into excess. That's the human condition. That snowballing takes up tremendous energy, uses valuable time, and hits us in a spot that we don't even realize— pride. Suddenly, we want a bigger car just so we can show off to our neighbors who don't really care what car we drive.

Stoic minimalism is about taming the excesses so that we come back to a mind that is undistracted by all that is petty. As such, minimalism serves two important purposes: (1) to stop possible distractions and (2) to place the mind on a higher trajectory.

However, there is a catch to all this. If you follow a list of things to do and get rid of that gets you to be a minimalist, then you have lost the plot. Completing your current situation and where you need to be is part of the process. If you have a Humvee as your vehicle, an onlooker may say that's an excess and tell you that that is the first thing you need to get rid of to be able to get on the path to being a minimalist. However, what if that Humvee were a source of your work? Let's say you are a tour guide in the tropical forests and you use that Humvee for guided tours. That Humvee, to you, is not an excess. That is why you cannot look at a geode book and get rid of the things they ask you to get rid of.

Instead, you need to look at all the things you do possess and ask yourself what purpose they have in your life. The key is matching its purpose to your purpose. Just like the man with the Humvee. For him, it's not an excess, but that same Humvee would not be for you if you live right across from your workplace and just need to cross the road to get here.

Your track toward minimalism is most likely going to be one that is gradual. You must not shock the system, but you should build your strength as you walk the path. Remember that you are building your wisdom as you take on this exercise as much as you are shunning distraction.

Stoic minimalism has a higher purpose. It is there to get you to contemplate your path and remove the layers of distraction that are around you. In time you will see that minimalism is not just applicable to tangible objects but also to intangible phenomena. For instance, you will start to realize that you do not need the adulation of your fellow man because you owe your pleasure to something of a higher order.

The heart of a Stoic is driven by his sense of duty first and foremost. His duty is not about serving any one man or group of people. This is a common misconception. You are not a slave to anyone, but neither are you lord over anyone either. You have a skill and intellect that is unique to you, and your sense of duty is to use that skill and intellect for the good of all those around you in any way you can. It is not to be proud of your ability but to be humble in its execution. It is not to receive praise for your ability but to know that you have to keep your head down and do more.

When Nathan Hale was captured in New York and executed, he said, "I only regret that I have but one life to give." It is not clear if he was Stoic, but that doesn't matter. No one is baptized into Stoicism or excommunicated from it. You are Stoic by the life you live, and Nathan Hale's mind-set after being caught by British troops indicates that he lived a life of duty for that in which he strongly believed—American independence.

Minimalism allows you to focus on the duty that you are uniquely designed to perform. If that sounds like a hint of socialism or communism since the greater good is achieved by contributing to others, then there is a missing facet in the understanding of one's presence in life. Duty is about what you give to everyone without expecting any measure of return except knowing that you have done what you were designed to do. In other words, you have served your purpose.

It so happens, however, that many modern-day Stoics have become very wealthy by doing their duty and contributing to society. In many cases, that works for a long time because they do not get distracted by the wealth; instead, they keep their heads down, shop at Target, and drive Toyotas.

To wrap up let's tie together some of the issues and the general themes in Stoicism so that you can bring minimalism into your life without wasting it on misunderstanding its power. If you blindly follow a to-do list and build a list of things that you have in your home to get rid of, you will waste the entire benefit of the exercise. You will look at the moment you gave all your things away and feel totally empty.

Instead, what you should do is look at each object in your possession and understand why you have it. The questions should be specific. If you are asking why you own a car, you should ask yourself why you own that specific car. Was there something lesser that you could have gotten? The answers have to be frank, honest, and consistent. Saying that you bought the car because you like it won't pass muster.

When you look at each object in your possession and pose these probing questions repeatedly and relentlessly, what you will inadvertently find is your own weaknesses and your own inconsistencies. If you have five coffee mugs that you use on a rotating basis, ask yourself why you have five. Why isn't one mug able to do the job?

When you whittle everything away by asking why you own something, you will find that you accumulate things that you don't need because you are trying to solve a deeper problem by association. If you have a lack of self-confidence, you may buy a bigger car regardless of how much debt you have to incur to do it. That car represents a need to compensate.

So, when you shine a light on it, you find insight into yourself. That insight is what makes the process toward minimalism so important and valuable. Don't trade that in for a meaningless list that tells you that you need to get rid of your car and take the bus, downsize your home and get an apartment, and wear cheaper clothes. You have to decide what is right for you—what you need to get rid of and why. That's the point of Stoic minimalism. It's the process, the intangible of the exercise—the so-called pneuma.

Until you do, getting rid of the object does you no good whatsoever.

Contemplation leading to minimalism is like teaching a child to not be afraid of the dark. You have to start with rationalizing the contents of the dark room and then go around the room and provide evidence that there is nothing under the bed or in the closet and then turn the lights off while holding their hands to assure them. At this point, you can introduce them to the concept of imagination. Just as the imaginative forces are confused with real observation in children, adults associate tangible things with intangible benefits that don't exist. For instance, how exactly does a Mercedes confer status in the mind of a stranger? What exactly are you hoping to get when you buy a BMW? When you buy a car, are you looking to get from A to B, or are you looking for pleasure?

Gradually, you start to see that it is all in your mind and that you don't need that Mercedes or BMW to make you happy. That's the real purpose of the contemplative process in Stoic minimalism. If you just decide, on a whim, after reading this or any other book to get rid of all that you have, it would have no benefit.

The train of thought in any reasoning process to adopt Stoic virtues is so that you find true and lasting happiness. However, the last thing you want to do in that process is to use a step-by-step guide to do it. Such guides are fine for making chocolate chip cookies but not for finding lifelong happiness.

Chapter 11 - Righteousness

"To righteousness, in speaking the truth freely,
and without ambiguity; and in doing all things
justly and discreetly. Now in this good course,
let not other men's either wickedness, or
opinion, or voice hinder thee: no, nor the sense
of this thy pampered mass of flesh: for let that
which suffers, look to itself."

— Meditations, Emperor Marcus Aurelius
Antoninus Augustus, 180AD

Speaking the truth does not stop at not telling lies. It is an entire array of conduct that exists on a plane. Being technical, yet misleading is not righteous. Being truthful but incomplete is not being righteous. And, being ambiguous for the purpose of evading the real question, yet not wanting to seem evasive is not righteous.

Being righteous is more than just the words we use or the quality of the representations we make. The words mean nothing if the actions that preceded them or followed them are flawed.

It comes back to the issue of wisdom. You have to have the wisdom to know when doing something is wrong. At the core of all this is that we are striving for happiness, and we gain the ultimate happiness by doing our duty.

Doing our duty to the world at large means we have to be virtuous in our conduct and honest in our thoughts, words, and deeds. Stoics, by advocating that happiness comes from virtue, automatically and explicitly embrace righteousness as well and find that it is a necessary condition to be able to be dutiful and thus gain happiness.

The problem that we so often face in the reality, however, is that our ambition, goals, and objectives come at odds to being dutiful, and it becomes more about selfishness and self-serving benefits at the expense of those to whom we owe our duty. When this happens, righteousness experiences fracture.

It has come to the point that we are willing to indulge in unrighteous acts and yet speak with honey potions on our lips to be able to cover the action that we think is warranted. We often act and then find that our actions deserve covering, and then we engage in lies and half-truths. These are all consequential issues and not the root of the matter.

The seed of destruction is planted when we slip from doing our duty and instead focus on serving our own needs and excesses. How do we know we are on that slippery slope? The only way to know is to ponder each action before it is executed. Knowing what you are doing is the key to being aware of your actions.

If you do not know the consequences of your action, then it is only right that you postpone that action until you have had time to evaluate and contemplate it. If you use all the faculties of your mind in the contemplation of your action(s) and find that it is righteous, then you should proceed to do it. If you execute what you can honestly say was a righteous action but it turns out to be detrimental, then you have to take responsibility for it, learn from it, and move on without regret. That is the method of a Stoic.

There are two veins to this happiness and thus to this matter on righteousness. In Stoic material, you find that happiness has a specific meaning. It is not being happy because you won the lottery; it is not being happy because your children got into an Ivy League institution. These are random events of joy and satisfaction, not happiness. Happiness is something more profound in Stoic philosophy. While this may all just seem like semantics if you practice the kind of happiness that Stoicism is advocating, you will see it reverberate across all the areas of your existence.

Stoic happiness is comprehensive and doesn't stop at being in harmony with the tangible world. It is about living in harmony with the intangible as well. Think back to our discussion about intangible and tangible aspects of all things.

Remember what the Stoics mean when it comes to nature. We saw in an earlier chapter that everything has its nature. We saw that we have the spirit of things or the pneuma. We also saw that there are tangible and intangible issues, and being one with nature means that you understand the object and the nature of things.

In other words, you have to observe it and absorb it. You can see with your eyes, but you have to observe with your mind. When you do that, you start to understand the nature of things.

It is worth pointing out that the nature we are talking about is not just limited to the trees and bugs that inhabit this planet or the stars and the cosmic bodies that share this universe with us. It is about how all things behave, and that includes how the mind works in the absence of virtue and how consequences affect lives down the road based on the original action.

Righteousness requires that one reflect and contemplate the reason for righteousness. Stoicism can't be understood by a how-to article or a cookbook-type approach. Every step of Stoicism needs to be looked at from scratch and taken into consideration and molded to fit each individual's life and situation.

The question then becomes: How does that reflect on the topic of righteousness? The word itself can mean different things to different people. Modern vernacular assigns a slightly different connotation to it, and classical translators who took the original meaning from the Greeks meant something else. Even this book has defined it for you, but you need to sit down and understand what it means to you by yourself.

To reflect on and contemplate righteousness requires that you trace back a given event in your life. Let's take, for instance, being stopped for DUI. It's not bad luck. If you take the sequence of events that got you to this point, you will start to understand righteousness.

You were stopped because you were driving erratically, or it was a random stop. The event that got you stopped is not the problem. If you were not legally drunk, the stop would have been uneventful. You were driving intoxicated because you were drinking. That in itself could be a problem because you should know ahead of time that if you are going to be drinking you shouldn't be driving and vice versa.

If you take it back one step and ask yourself why you didn't think of things that way, you may find that you felt your desires or habits more important to fulfill than taking the risk with your life or breaking the law.

The key to back-tracing is to look back on the event and see where the root of that chain of events lies. In this case, it could go all the way back to the habit of drinking, or it could go all the way back to driving. If you look hard enough, you may decide to stop drinking or stop driving and get on the rideshare bandwagon. Both of which would be righteous in this case.

The key to contemplating righteousness is to not stop at reflecting on the event immediately preceding an unfortunate consequence but to throw back all the way to the genesis of the train of events. If you go back to the root of that chain of events, you may even realize that it has other possible consequences as well.

This hypothetical assumes that you contemplate righteousness in the wake of a problem. So, what about other times when something has not caused deep consequence? What if it is still lurking and waiting to rear its head?

This is when contemplation of all your actions, over time, comes in. If you look at all the things in your life and trace them back to the genesis act or thought process, then what you will find is the ability to define a set of righteous acts and thoughts.

You don't have to think about these in moral or immoral terms when you get started. Morality is a very different train of thought than righteousness. At this point in the book and in the shadow of Stoicism, we are not looking at right and wrong, moral or immoral. We are looking at the consequences of your life based on an action. The previous example had a little bit about legislation (DUI) mixed in, but that is not the focal point of the example. Do not mix up laws with righteousness. There are unrighteous laws, as Gandhi used to say. Righteousness has to do with nature and doing right by it. In return, you will find the peace and happiness that will elude you elsewhere.

One of the most common elements of righteousness is the concept of telling the truth. There are various benefits to this downstream.

The first is that telling the truth all the time gives you the peace of mind you need so that you do not have to keep track of the lies you tell.

More importantly, telling lies has un upstream complication, meaning that it can gravitate up to matters that precede the lie.

Let's look at this a little closer so as to not confuse the matter. If you lie and get away with it, your mind learns a new skill. It learns the art of getting away with lies. That's not always a good thing. It may have short-term benefits, but the long term is never good. Here is where the upstream issue comes in. If you start getting to the point that you can lie well, you will be inclined to do things that are not good because you know that you can lie about it later.

So, in essence, the ability to lie erodes your hesitancy to do things that go against the nature of things. If you steal someone's money and lie about it and get away with it, it will embolden you to steal again.

There are two kinds of truth-telling that you should be concerned with. The first is about telling the truth about things within your own gravity. If you did something wrong, you should own up to it. That way, you wouldn't have to lie about it, and, in the future, you wouldn't be emboldened to do more wrong acts.

Telling the truth works upstream and downstream. Stoics realize this from the very beginning and are not accustomed to lying or living a lie. There is a distinction in those two conditions. Telling a lie is the part where you speak falsely, but living a lie is when you live under the consequences of maintaining that lie, and that in many cases is significantly worse. Stoicism speaks furiously against this kind of life.

When Cato the Younger battled Caesar, he did so to protect Rome from possible tyranny. He had seen Caesar's ambition and had determined to block any attempt to slow-walk his beloved country into the hands of a dictator. He did it out of a sense of duty toward a greater purpose, and that signifies his adherence to the core of Stoicism. When his armies lost the attempt to check Caesar's army, Cato was certain that

Caesar would have him killed. But Caesar didn't have him killed but instead pardoned his rebellion. If he accepted that pardon, it would have meant that Cato would have to live a lie for the rest of his life. He knew that he would be forced to swear allegiance to Caesar—an allegiance that would be a lie. Instead of succumbing to that position, he committed suicide. That's how much living in truth meant to Stoics. Of course, today, it would be looked upon as ridiculous, but no one is asking us to do that right now, and most of us are not in that kind of position. But it is still wise to measure the weight of truth with Cato's example and see the relative importance it should have in our daily life.

Righteousness doesn't stop at just telling the truth. Righteousness blankets the existence of the Stoic with a sense of an all-pervading shield. It blankets the Stoic from reproach, it protects him from intimidation, it gives him the gravity of the righteous, and it imbues confidence because when he is righteous, he becomes imperturbable.

That shield is the ultimate state of strength. It can't be stolen, beaten, or incarcerated.

Chapter 12 - A Stoic's Individuality

"I have often wondered how it should come to pass, that every man loving himself best, should more regard other men's opinions concerning himself than his own."

— Meditations, Emperor Marcus Aurelius Antoninus Augustus, 180AD

There is a long-standing debate on whether Stoicism promotes individualism or collectivism. The debate is moot because the issue was actually settled more than two thousand years ago, but it is not hard to see why it is still misunderstood today.

On one side of the coin, much of the philosophy and ideology of the Stoic is based on improving the self and increasing one's awareness and one's righteousness. The four virtues of Stoicism—wisdom, justice, courage, and temperance—are all decidedly matters that are for the individual to handle within himself.

Some even go so far as to claim that Stoics should evangelize and force others to take on the righteous path of a Stoic. But this is wrong. There is no evangelization in Stoicism, just as you cannot learn to be Stoic from a how-to book. Evangelizing doesn't work in Stoicism because Stoicism is an experience and not a membership. Stoicism comes from inside after much contemplation, reflection, and meditation. It doesn't come after being lectured. If you have the opportunity to observe a Stoic, you will be able to learn more by what you see him do than by what you hear him say. That makes evangelizing impossible.

Then there is the other side of the coin. The sense of duty that we have looked at repeatedly thus far has a strange reflection of collectivism. This is probably why the debate is not a settled issue in some circles. To the untrained eye, there seems to be shades of individualism in some corners of Stoic thought, and there seems to be shades of collectivism in others.

The best way to look at this is a proverb that is told in Buddhist ashrams in the East. It fits the situation at hand perfectly:

Some time ago there was a father and daughter team of acrobats in a Chinese circus. The father would hoist the daughter on his shoulders, while she would balance herself on him and spin plates at the end of a stick. If either lost their footing, both would tumble onto each other to a catastrophic end. The father, worried about his daughter, kept telling her to be careful. His concern, while being a distraction to her, reduced his focus. After each act, she would tell him to not worry about her, and his response was that he was just doing his duty to look after her. In his mind, he was to look after her, and she was to look after him.

To this, she replied, "That is not the best way, father. If you worry about me and I worry about you, we will both make mistakes, and both of us will fall. But if I focus fully on what I have to do, and you focus fully on what you have to do, we will both turn out all right."

If both practiced individualism, their duty to each other would be fulfilled.

In the same vein as that parable, Stoics are arduous in their focus on what they do as individuals while knowing in the back of their mind that when they do that the whole would work out better.

Thus, the question comes back to whether Stoics are individualists or collectivists. At this point, the answer should be clear. We are both. We stand with the notion that we have the duty to serve, but we are not our brother's keeper.

To serve, in duty, we know that we have to have the wisdom to be able to provide justice, courage, and temperance. In turn, to have wisdom, we have to keep our eye and mind on the world around us and sharpen our minds. That is why the Stoics were the ones behind grammar and thought that it was paramount in the observation and dissemination of information and data.

That brings us back to individuality.

The pursuit of individuality is just as important as the attainment and practice of individuality. Individuality dovetails into a number of other areas in a person's life. When you think about standing up as an individual, you are looking at how to make your life your own and not following the opinions and judgment of others. Stoics don't care what others think of them. The extreme of this you could see in Diogenes (although he wasn't a Stoic; he was a Cynic). The strain of the Cynic school of thought that made it into the initial thoughts of Zeno and the subsequent foundations of Stoicism is that a person's character is strongest when they have no need to hold on to the expectations of others.

Individualism in Stoics is not about being alone or being isolated. It is about the strength of being independent and the strength to not be swayed by what others think. You can't live your life by poll numbers.

The stature of individuality is clasped by two polar requirements. On one side is the requirement of strength. Strength, in this sense, is not the muscles one flexes but the strength of righteousness. On the other side is the requirement of humility or the total lack of arrogance. It is easy to slip into arrogant states when pursuing the stature of individuality. While it is common to speak against that arrogance, it is not as common as finding the best way to go about it.

Practicing Stoics tend to deal with arrogance and promote humility within themselves by striking a balance between talking and listening. Shakespeare writes in Hamlet, "give every man thy ear, but few thy voice." It is the ultimate memory aid in thinking what a Stoic would do when confronted with the opportunity to be arrogant about not listening to another's opinion. Listening, just like seeing, is not something that you do with your senses but with your mind. Merely seeing with your eyes and hearing with your ears is not the way to go about "giving every man their ear."

Merely listening to their words will get you nowhere and will only waste your time. Listening with your mind, however, will give you insight into a number of things that you can't predict before you hear what someone else has to say.

That practiced gradually turns to a state where they know that much of what a person has to say may be irrelevant to the life of the Stoic in question, but, nonetheless, somewhere in the haystack, he may find the proverbial needle, and that is worth the effort. That renders the Stoics humble or at least be able to stand without arrogance.

Marcus Aurelius wrote in his journal, which was posthumously published under the title *Meditations*, that when one arises in the morning he or she should remind themselves that the day would be filled with all kinds of people coming up with all kinds of issues and problems, saying all kinds of things, and making all kinds of criticisms.

The goal of the Stoic is to not allow any of it to penetrate the shield of righteousness, yet patiently listen to what they have to say, and in the event there is something worthy in it, to add it to their own repertoire of knowledge so that they may tread forward enriched and enlightened.

Imagine for a moment if Zeno of Citium decided to walk away from a rambling man who claimed to speak of things previously unheard of. If Zeno didn't stop to listen to them, he wouldn't have had the opportunity to meet with Crates of Thebes, who taught him about the Cynic school of thought, and that sparked Zeno's thought process.

So now you have two sides of the individuality coin. On one side is the strength you need to stand on your own principles, thoughts, and actions. On the other side, you have the humility to be able to give someone your mind's ear.

Once that is done, the Stoic still has one more element in his armor that comes into play. It is the armor of contemplation and reflection. However strange or inane a person's position, if you look at it in its entirety, or if you look at it with your mind and understand what he or she is purporting, you will find that it makes sense on some level, and it will make sense to you. In other words, there will be something that you can benefit from it when you subject it to your mind.

Rene Descartes, the French philosopher, who was also a student of Stoic teachings, extends this individuality when he teaches the way one should hold another's words. He advocates listening to them and suspending your own beliefs and ideas even to the point of suspending your own reality while you listen clearly to what this other person has to say. Then while you have suspended your own view on the matter, investigate this new piece of information with fresh and unbiased eyes. When you are done, you have one of three courses of action to take. You can replace your belief and ideals with what you just learned. Or, you can reject the new idea but realize that there are those who still see this issue in a certain way. Or, finally, you can look at some of the issues that were in the idea, and some of the foundation of it could be used by you in your thinking.

There is nothing that anyone can say that has zero benefits to you if you listen and think carefully. A Stoic knows this. If you speak to a

Stoic, you can be sure that he will listen to all that you have to say, process it, and respond without ego and bluster no matter how opposed to the idea he may be.

Chapter 13 - Death & Stoicism

"How ridiculous and strange is he, that wonders at anything that happens in this life in the ordinary course of nature!"

— *Meditations, Emperor Marcus Aurelius Antoninus Augustus, 180AD*

We end this book with a topic that is taboo in most conversations—one that concerns one's own mortality. Human beings, while they are hardwired to protect themselves and have the fear of death as a feature of their minds, are subjected to consequential and sometimes negative ripple effects from it.

The pleasures of life, the heartache of parting from loved ones, the thought of the ache in the life of those loved ones, not to mention the inherent fear of the unknown state, are all powerful reasons to fear physical death.

Stoics see death very differently from most philosophes in the East and West and differently from many of the major religions practiced today. To put it unceremoniously, Stoics see death as a natural extension of life. Because it is a natural extension of life, death, in itself, has zero impact on what a Stoic says and does.

In that same vein, Stoics see their responsibility to remain alive for as long as naturally possible as part of their duty so that they can be of service for the longest amount of time possible.

In Stoicism, there are two kinds of death. One is physical death, which is death that comes when the mind and body are no longer able to show signs of any life. The second is when the person's use to his fellow man around him has ceased. Remember again that a Stoic's life is in duty to the world at large. Total incapacitation to a Stoic is tantamount to death.

That incapacity could come as mental incapacity or physical incapacity, but in many cases, it even comes as intellectual incapacity or the incapacity to execute one's principles. Take the deaths of Cato the Younger and Brutus the Younger as an example.

That then begs the question. Does it mean that once a person is no longer able to perform his duty he is better off dead? Yes. But a person who is alive can find many ways to do a duty to the rest of his brethren; he just has to find it.

On the other hand, what about one's desire to keep one's self healthy and alive? Is that the wrong thing for a Stoic to do? No. It is the Stoic's duty to remain alive for as long as he can and to keep himself as healthy as he can so that he may be of service for as long as possible to as many as possible.

There is a lot of writing that weighs and discusses this topic in Stoic philosophy. Listing each one is beyond the scope of this book, especially when we can easily surmise the point that it all boils down to.

It comes back to the prospect of death being a powerful force in our life. Imagine if you were to live forever. Would you be motivated to do anything? It's like getting to a vacation destination and saying that you are going to live there indefinitely. Would you rush out of the hotel room as soon as you check in so that you can catch the sights on your first day there? No, you'd take your time.

It is the same with life. The idea that you are going to be here indefinitely would cause you to take it easy with things and not try to be all you can be or do all you could do. The knowledge of a finite present in this realm of living should make you want to spend more time absorbing all this level of consciousness allows.

Stoics realize that death is the greatest teacher and the greatest tool a person has if they are willing to contemplate it forward. When you fear death, have you asked yourself as a Stoic does, what is it that you fear? All questions that come in the wake of that question have a different flavor in their answer.

What do people who fear death actually fear? Is it pain? It can't be because there is no pain upon death, which by its very definition renders the senses nonexistent and thus the inability to feel pain. So, what is it to you? As a neophyte, you have to contemplate death to a degree that you are able to see it or what it is. If you are just starting out in Stoicism, this is a good place to start.

As a sidebar, to stress the level of importance that is inherent in the need for you to contemplate your own mortality, let us do a thought experiment. Imagine the color yellow. Now imagine having to explain that color using words alone to a person who has been blind all his life. How would you do it?

You wouldn't be able to get very far. Something similar happens in our quest to explain death in the context of living. We use the concept of beginning and end to denote points in a timeline, but to say that it is the end is not accurate. Stoics see it as a change in tangible circumstances because the pneuma is still intact. In death, the tangible ceases, but the intangible remains.

Language and conversations have limitations that preclude the communication of certain kinds of information. The only way to approach that information would be to contemplate it and/or to experience it. In the same way, the topic of death is not something that can be described but is something that can be contemplated.

It is natural to fear death. We naturally fear the unknown. All Stoics start in the same way as those outside the congregation of this philosophy. The difference is that Stoics start to weigh the matter by looking at that duty as the reason for them to maintain their life to the greatest extent possible but not an inch further. By focusing on duty and not death, they no longer fear it.

If fear overly animates our thoughts about something that is inevitable but not in the moment, then that fear has done more to harm than protect us. The fear of death when there is no logical and discernable reason or danger is not productive, and this is a distraction to the effective contemplation of all things.

To take up the life of a Stoic, contemplating death before you contemplate the other matters that have been discussed in this book will give you the necessary tools to extend all the other teachings, principles, and ideas that Stoicism has to offer.

Putting your life in order is wise so that it reduces your subconscious concerns that there are things that you have to fulfill but have not yet done. What one may fear is not fear of the unknown on the other side of death but rather the projected fear of not fulfilling one's duties on this side of death.

If that is the case, one has to focus on the fact that there is no time to waste, no time for idle chatter, no frivolous pleasures of the flesh, and certainly no time to be inefficient. These are all the things that you have to put in order posthaste.

Conclusion

The best way to get to know something is to dive straight into it, make mistakes, have misunderstandings, seek advice, and then spend the bulk of your time contemplating it and integrating it with one's own life experiences.

The conversation about Stoic virtues that is facing its renaissance in our lifetime has become vibrant over the last decade and more so in the last three years. Whether that indicates that the pendulum of human consciousness has swung from its apex in religious belief and disappointment or that we are just looking for answers in a world that has so many challenges is a contemplative proposition.

During this period of Stoic renaissance, it is worth our while to understand the genesis and the circumstances that existed in that time and the trajectory of events before Zeno landed in Athens. The point was that man has been looking to find his divinity. Whether it was placing his time in pursuing sanctioned religion from Christianity to Islam or unsanctioned beliefs from paganism to witchcraft, man has been on a quest to place meaning to life that goes from cradle to grave.

Therein lies the problem. He has limited his quest to between two distinct points in the journey—the day he was born and the day he will die.

Most teachings have failed to answer the question that percolates deep within when they only seem to intimate a limited purpose and a limited scope of life, but Stoics in their collective methods and plain pursuit of wisdom have opened a way for us to stretch our lives beyond the bookends of physical birth and physical death.

Life is more than that. It is not a drop in time. It is a continuum that extends from the point of the universe's creation and will continue while we evolve into higher and better forms of consciousness. There is no end to this just as your day doesn't end just because you turn in for the night.

Stoicism is not a set of rules and dogmas. In fact, it is not a fixed set of instructions for the way you should live your life. It is a compendium of thoughts and experiences that you can use. You do not need to be certified or experience a ritual to be inducted as a Stoic; in fact, you may already be one just by the way you conduct your life.

Gandhi was not a Stoic by admission, but his life and pursuit of duty and righteousness provide clear evidence of a life steeped in Stoic values. His wisdom and sense of justice for all applied with unshakeable courage and devout temperance at all times speaks volumes about what it is like to live a Stoic life.

The question remains, however, if happiness in the way it is defined in Stoic circles is something that resonates within you when you hear about it. If it does, then the path through Stoic values would be something that you can benefit from, and it will not detract from whatever religious beliefs that you may already have. In fact, it may give you the perspective you need to extract better value from it.

If, however, you don't see the point of Stoicism, then you should ask yourself which area of Stoic virtue is not vibrating with your inherent frequency. There is nothing wrong with not wanting to be Stoic, but not jiving with it is an opportunity for self-learning and getting to know yourself. At the very least, this book should place you on a path that will result in learning about who you are, what you are made of, and how that would turn out for you in the future.

When we look at life and compare it with the symphony, we see that the best way for all the parts to work is for each to follow its own purpose—just like the symphony and the father and daughter acrobats in the parable. To make sure the collective works, Stoics need to be highly individualistic, which requires focusing on improving the tangible and intangible aspects of one's existence.

Your desire to know about Stoicism may just be simple curiosity, or it may be the deep desire to fulfill the potential that is locked up inside you. Stoic practice is one of the most effective ways and efficient means to unlock the potential of the human mind and unleash the power of the soul.

If you enjoyed learning about Stoicism, I would be forever grateful if you could leave a review on Amazon. Reviews are the best way to provide feedback to newer authors like myself. It also helps your fellow readers so make sure to help them out! Thanks so much.

-   Kyle Faber

Printed in Great Britain
by Amazon

82058806R00123